Sam and Nia

Public Scandal | Secret Vows | Restored Hearts

Live in Truth

Our Memoir
By Samuel and Nia Rader

Nisam Media Inc.

Sam and Nia | Live in Truth
© 2024 by Samuel and NiaChel Rader. All rights reserved.

No portion of this book may be reproduced, stored in a retrieval system, or transmitted in any form or by any means—electronic, mechanical, photocopy, recording, scanning, or other—except for brief quotations in critical reviews or articles, without the prior written permission of the publisher.

Self Published in Rockwall, Texas,
by Samuel and Nia Rader of Nisam Media Inc.

Cover Design: Samuel Rader
Cover photograph: Matthew Rader: matthewtrader.com
Back cover portrait: Matthew Rader

Special editorial thanks: Michael Rader, Matthew Rader, Jeffrey Streutker, Sara Chambers, the Dausters, and Caleb Fauber

All Scripture quotations, unless otherwise indicated, are taken from:
Holy Bible: English Standard Version (ESV). © 2016 by Crossway Bibles, Wheaton, IL. All rights reserved.
Holy Bible: New Living Translation (NLT). © 2015 by Tyndale House Publishers, Carol Stream, IL. All rights reserved.
Holy Bible: New International Version (NIV). © 2011 by Zondervan, Grand Rapids, MI. All rights reserved.

For more information, please e-mail info@samandnia.com

Copyright © 2024 Samuel and NiaChel Rader

All rights reserved.

ISBN: 9798867502881

Disclosure

- This memoir reflects our personal experiences and memories as accurately as we could recall. Although the core and vast majority of the details are true to our lives, certain aspects, such as conversations, have been modified for clarity and brevity or to more effectively convey lessons learned and to enhance the narrative.
- Most names have been changed to protect the identity of the guilty.
- This book includes descriptions of adult situations that many may find inappropriate for children under the age of 16.
- This content may be highly triggering for couples who are healing from or have gone through infidelity.

Dedicated to our children

Symphony, you weren't aware of it, but you were our sidekick through all of the hard times and good times depicted in this book. You were growing up and learning about love and life right along with us. I pray that our story and the lessons we learned with you by our side will one day help you when you need it most.

Abram, you brought us many needed breaks from the sadness described in this book, giving us a reason to smile and laugh when nothing else could. We pray that the patience you showed us while writing this book will one day pay off for you as a future husband, father, and man of God.

Juliet, as you'll see in these pages, it's no wonder you're such a fan of love and romance. You entered our lives just as we were grasping the greatest romance of all time: the gospel. You are a living picture of that beautiful time for us. We pray you will always allow God's love to shine through you and inspire many.

Josie, you bring a unique, bonding excitement to our family. As we all adore and treasure your amazing personality, it brings us closer to each other and strengthens our family. We pray that you will continue to embrace life boldly and utilize your unifying gift to glorify God and advance His church.

Contents

Part 1
Dawn of Deliverance
(1.5 years before full confession)

1. In the News 11
2. Frozen Yogurt 15
3. Meet Cutie 19
4. Pulling Curtains 25
5. First Class 31
6. CPS 35

Part 2
Through the Wilderness
(Weeks before full confession)

7. Rings and Results 43
8. Muffled Joy 49
9. Viral Again 53
10. Handful of Tears 57

Part 3
Burned, Not Consumed
(Days before full confession)

11. Rumored Remorse 63
12. Ashley Madison 67
13. Shattered 73
14. Daddy's Not Home 79
15. Untying the Knot 85
16. Tempo Change 91
17. Mocking Forgiven 95

Part 4
Parted Waters
(The full confession)

18. Live in Truth 101
19. Peace Illusion 107
20. Trust Fall 111
21. Nightmare Drive 117
22. Unsnared 123
23. Calling Jane 127
24. Self-Mutilation 131

Part 5
Mirages and Manna
(Aftermath of confession)

25. Missed Flight 139
26. Life Sentence 143
27. Redhead at Walmart 149
28. The Guardrail 153
29. One-Night Stand 159
30. Sex Ed 163
31. Final Indecision 167
32. Holey Blouse 173
33. Shiny Boxes 177
34. Temptation Test 181
35. Pestilence 185

Part 6
Eden Reclaimed
(The final confession)

36. Wake-Up Crash 193
37. Broke 199
38. The Diagnosis 203
39. Joyful Heartache 207
40. Can't Rewind 213
41. Fully Exposed 217
42. Leaving Home 221
43. Final Confession 225
44. Once a Cheater 229
45. Ultimate Romance 237

Foreword
Bo Dauster

Hey there, I'm Bo. I know we haven't officially met, but believe me when I tell you you are in for an intense and unparalleled journey. The following story is packed full of some of the most extreme emotional experiences a person could ever face.

This story features romance, devotion, fame, family, betrayal, heartbreak, forgiveness, unique adventures, persisting doubts, God's healing, and the power and pains of living in truth. But, as with many of the best stories, this is ultimately about love and how it is the light that guides you home when you've somehow gotten so lost.

To most people who know their names, Sam and Nia are smiling faces that bring little bits of joy and laughter through their YouTube videos. But to me, they are flesh and blood. We've prayed, taken vacations, laughed, wept, healed, built a church, and watched our children grow up together.

In this book, you will get to know Sam and Nia more deeply than even their entire archive of vlogs could reveal. As their story unfolds, I believe their raw and uncensored authenticity will bless you as they take you through their one-of-a-kind life experiences. No matter what you're facing in life, I'm confident there will be something in their story that will be a lasting encouragement to you.

Like I said, buckle up because it's going to be an intense ride.

Live in Truth

Prologue
Netflix

*Their feet run to evil... but these men lie in wait for their own blood;
they set an ambush for their own lives.
Proverbs 1:16-18*

(Sam)

"WHAT MADE YOU agree to do this interview?" asked Toby, the director, perched on a stool in my garage, two bulky Netflix cameras capturing every detail of my expressions.

"Oh, I knew this day would come," I said without hesitation.

Although I had no idea I'd get an opportunity to share our story on the world's largest paid streaming service, I always knew that one way or another, I'd publicly confront the lies I told to millions of people after the Ashley Madison (AM) breach.

I had been waiting nine years for this moment to arrive; however, in May 2022, when we first received the email from Minnow Films, Nia and I were uncertain about participating in their AM docuseries. In fact, we had already declined a request from ABC to participate in their documentary on the same subject, which later went to Paramount+ (we dodged a bullet with that decision).

The email from Minnow Films read:

Dear Sam and Nia, I hope this email finds you well. I'm

Prologue

> *writing to you from Minnow Films… to let you know about a documentary series we are currently developing for a prominent global streaming service about the Ashley Madison data breach in 2015. …it would be our aspiration to collaborate closely with victims who were impacted by what happened and have overcome the challenges presented by the media attention that came with the story. With that in mind, I very much hoped you might be open to having an initial conversation about your experiences.*

Years before this email, I had made a promise to myself: if I were ever to speak publicly about my leaked AM account again, I would address the lies I told in my initial response and provide a fuller picture of my brokenness, Nia's forgiveness, and God's redemptive work in our marriage.

After further correspondence, Nia and I learned that Minnow Films planned to feature our story alongside those of many others affected by the breach, with our part reduced to a few snippets in a single episode. While it was great they wanted to give a voice to so many affected by the hack, the chances that they'd make room for us to even begin to touch on the full scope of our complicated story were slim to none.

Given this knowledge, on top of our existing plans to write a book, we felt that participating in the docuseries might not be the right choice. Not to mention, my brother Matthew had already begun a documentary of his own, exclusively focused on our story that he had every intention of one day completing.

I wrote Minnow Films, "Our story is just too complex to be covered in a single interview. It's so much bigger than just the Ashley Madison breach." I explained further that our story required much more context than what we understood their project would cover.

"Besides," I added, "Jesus is the center of our story, and we want it to remain that way… I know many people in this industry can be offended by Jesus." We were doubtful that Netflix would accurately portray the most crucial aspect of our story: God's redemption. Yet the producers persisted despite my stubbornness.

After further persuasion, I agreed to an off-the-record call with Billy at Minnow Films to hear more about their proposal. Following our conversation, Billy kindly requested that I write him an email detailing more of our story, saying, "Your story is very compelling, and I agree; it needs to be told." He added, "And the spiritual aspect of it is a very important part."

Although I felt he was just telling me what I wanted to hear, I was more than willing to share my testimony with him, as I was with anyone interested in hearing it. I wrote him a 942-word brief account of how the AM breach had forever changed Nia's and my life.

"You articulate your experiences extremely well," he responded, "and I really appreciate the honesty and raw emotion. Let me take this to the team and get back to you."

Following several more exchanges, during which Nia and I were promised that our story would be accurately represented if we agreed to sit in front of their cameras, we gradually became more open to the idea of participating.

Before long, we found ourselves on a Zoom call with the casting directors, Claire and Amanda, to give it more consideration. "So why don't we start with the breach itself," Fiona suggested, "how you as a couple confronted that and worked through it?"

"It was an insane flip of being on the most incredible high of success of my entire life," I explained, "to being at the absolute lowest point of my life."

As Claire and Fiona's genuine interest in our story deepened, they asked if we'd start from the beginning, from when we first met in high school to the moment we found ourselves thrust into the limelight.

Nia and I spent the next two hours laughing and crying as we shared how God miraculously transformed our marriage through a YouTube channel in a series of otherworldly twists and turns.

After several subsequent interviews with the Minnow Films team, they agreed that our story was "too vast" and "too compelling" to be condensed into snippets in a single episode.

"Your story will be the heartbeat of the series," Toby, the director, informed us. He shared that they had even excluded other stories they were keen on telling to allocate more time to ours.

After reaching further agreements, we entered into a contract with Minnow Films.

"Okay, Sam," Toby said, nodding to the sound guy as he turned off the loudly humming AC window unit in my garage. "Thanks for that. Now, let's circle back to the moment you and Nia created your very first viral hit."

PART 1
Dawn of Deliverance
1.5 years before full confession

1
On the News

Be sober-minded; be watchful. Your adversary, the devil, prowls around like a roaring lion, seeking someone to devour.
1 Peter 5:8

(Sam)

I WAS RUSHING BETWEEN patients. Filling the ER was the constant sound of beeping monitors, pump alarms, and call lights when I heard someone call out my name.

"Sam!?" a woman's voice shouted. I stopped and turned my head toward an admin sitting behind her desk. "Is that you on the news?!" she exclaimed, gesturing toward the mounted TV in front of her.

The ER erupted in gasps and whispers as my co-workers looked at the TV screen and then back at me, their eyes wide in disbelief. My heart leaped in my chest as I saw my wife's and my faces staring back at me on a screen behind Savannah Guthrie and Al Roker on the Today Show.

"Oh my gosh," I said under my breath. "That's us, alright." It was close to the end of my shift, about 6:30 AM. A lip-sync video Nia and I had filmed inside our Honda Pilot and posted to YouTube only the day before was making the early morning news.

After the brief spectacle of watching their co-worker's name come out of the mouths of some of the most famous people in America, the staff returned to their tasks as though nothing unusual had happened. Little did they know, however, that I was undergoing a profound inner metamorphosis. The usual cloud of discontentment for my job that hovered over me for the past two years was receding right before their eyes.

I felt a huge pull between my professional duties as a registered nurse and the realization that my long-forgotten dream of becoming famous was suddenly becoming a reality. I slipped into a vacant treatment room and slid the door and curtain closed behind me. I sat on the edge of the bed and let my thoughts swirl chaotically.

Could this be my way out of nursing? I wondered. *I have to tell Nia. Is my life going to be exciting after all!?*

My friends and family were well aware of my "rock band" in high school called *Free the Float,* and the first song we wrote and recorded called *All We Want is Fame.* It was a laughable memory. Yet, there I was, a 28-year-old nurse, feeling like that same 17-year-old, attention-hungry class clown again. Then, an impactful conversation I had with a youth pastor during that period resurfaced in my memory.

"Without a father figure to make you feel seen and heard," my youth pastor explained, "you probably missed out on approval as a child, leading to a craving for external validation, something fame appears to promise." I had admitted to him that it seemed I was constantly dreaming about being applauded by a large audience.

Just as I was about to unlock my phone to see if Nia was awake and tell her that we were on the morning news, I fell into a trance-like state as a somber memory of my father flashed through my mind.

****

My dad pivoted in his seat, making eye contact with me, sitting on the rubber floor in the back of his company work van.

"Stay here; I'll be back in five minutes," he instructed. Dad exited the van, giving his belt a tug and his beeper a press, then closed his door.

I hopped into the vacated driver's seat, mimicking his usual driving position: right hand on the steering wheel, left elbow on the window ledge. *This is how Dad drives,* I thought. Given his limited verbal communication with me, I knew his body language well.

I watched the back of Dad's fluffy white hair as he fed coins into a payphone outside our local Dollar General. As he held the receiver to his ear, a familiar back-and-forth shifting of his body weight told me he was agitated. I didn't think much of it. We were all accustomed to his short temper and unpredictable flare-ups. However, my interest was piqued when his gaze swept across the parking lot, and I spotted a smile on his face, persisting even as he talked. He fiddled with the door of the coin return, then combed his fingers through his hair, letting out a big laugh. He was radiating with a giddiness I didn't recognize.

I leaned over the steering wheel and despite sensing he was talking to a woman who wasn't my mom. I found my smile mirroring his. Growing up, I'd seen Dad shoulder more burdens than joy, seemingly always stressed out. The weariness in his eyes had always hinted at dreams put off and quiet sacrifices made for the sake of our family. Witnessing this sliver of joy, this lightness in his demeanor while talking to someone who brought a genuine smile to his face, my childish heart couldn't help but feel happy for him. Days later, however, he pushed that deceived young man too far, and my joy turned into feelings of betrayal.

We were on our way home from watching my oldest brother Matthew graduate from Army boot camp in Alabama when Dad took my other brothers and me for breakfast at a strange woman's house in the dark hours of the morning. He gathered us around her dining room table as she served us pancakes in her red bathrobe.

Despite the discomfort, fully aware of this woman's relationship with Dad, I uttered words I'll always regret: "Our mom never makes us pancakes like this," I said, aiming to impress Dad. He responded with a reassuring nod and a grin.

As we drove the rest of the way home that morning, my remark ate away at me, making me feel complicit in his cheating. As we rolled into the driveway of our house, I wanted to gag up the pancakes at the thought of facing Mom inside.

Sitting on the bed where Mom lay, I updated her on the events of the past few days we spent without her. "Did you guys do anything on your way home?" she asked.

I looked down at the floor and quietly replied, "He took us to a lady's house for breakfast."

She sat up in the bed and screamed, "What!?" After giving Mom more details, she sprang up, stormed out of the room, and confronted Dad. I listened to them shout curse words at each other at the top of their lungs and thought, *Maybe if they get all the anger out now, things will get better.*

"Get out of my house, you pig!" Mom demanded.

As they continued screaming at each other, my twin brother and I dashed upstairs to our bedroom, giggling as if we were playing a fun game of hide-and-seek. From our hiding spots, we heard the muffled sound of Dad stomping up the stairs.

"Michael and Samuel, where are you?!" he screamed. Once in our bedroom, he ripped the covers off me, exposing a terrified boy stuffed in the fetal position between the top bunk of our bed and wall, then yanked my twin brother out of our closet by his shirt. Pulling back his fist, he screamed, "Do you see what you caused?!"

He left us guilt-stricken in our room as he packed up his belongings and left, never to set foot in our home again, leaving Mom with a broken heart and five bereft children to raise on her own.

****

During my twenty-minute drive home from the hospital, an hour after seeing my face on live television, a comment left on our video repeatedly echoed in my mind. "Very entertaining," it read. "Sam, you are in the wrong profession." The comment confirmed what I had been telling myself for years: I was meant for something else.

When I arrived home, so lost in thought on the drive that I barely remembered the journey, I burst through the front door, ran into the kitchen, and exclaimed with my arms playfully raised above my head, "This is it, cutie! My prayers have been answered!"

Nia leaped into my arms and screamed, "I can't believe it!" Her voice was full of emotion. "It's already at 2 million views!"

Nia was fully aware of how my job as an ER nurse had worn on me and the depressive thoughts it led to. She was my biggest cheerleader, always willing to sacrifice anything at the drop of a hat if it meant I could pursue what I love. Nia assumed that all my decisions were also made with our family's best interests in mind, believing I was just as devoted and sacrificial as she was. At that moment, that was indeed the truth.

2
Frozen Yogurt

*Keep your heart with all vigilance,
for from it flow the springs of life.
Proverbs 4:23*

(Nia)

ON A SPRING AFTERNOON, three days after uploading our lip-sync video, Sam and I, and our two children, left the house to grab a treat: some "frozen" yogurt. Walking from our car towards Sweet Frogs, a boy among a group of teenagers crossing our path looked up at us and yelled, "Hey, aren't y'all that *Frozen* couple!?"

Sam laughed. "That sounds like us!" He yelled back.

"That was an epic video," he said.

I slapped Sam's arm and squealed, "Did you hear that? Little ole us! Being recognized as the *Frozen* couple!"

I enjoyed the sudden popularity, but more so, I enjoyed watching Sam get recognition for something creative he had put his heart into. Not to mention, the very idea of him being recognized on the streets likely had him ecstatic inside.

The moment was reminiscent of the early days of our relationship when Sam wanted to take his high-school punk band to California in hopes of becoming famous. I was his number-one fan, soon-to-be groupie, and the girl he wrote all his love songs about.

Sam had already made my dreams come true simply by making me feel like I belonged, adoring and loving me in a way no one ever had. And then, of course, there was him making me his wife and starting a family with me, making all my pretend play as a child and my teenage fantasies an amazing reality.

Growing up, I never had the luxury of a doting, let alone committed, man in my life. However, the allure of fame and fortune, much like the dreams Sam had, was familiar territory for me. It formed the backdrop to the very beginning of my life.

****

At 24 years old, still living with her mom in Texas, my mother packed up her things and headed to California for adventure and excitement. There, she met a fame-hungry singer for a semi-popular rock band called *London*. It was while traveling the globe and partying with this "rockstar" that my mom became pregnant with me.

After learning that she was expecting, she returned home to my grandmother and got clean from drugs and alcohol. As for my father, he wanted nothing to do with a baby and continued his pursuit of fame without us. We never heard from him again.

I was born on September 2, 1988, in a small Texas town called Kaufman. My mom gave me the French name NiaChel Jonique, but it wasn't long before I was simply called Nia. With my name given but never fully embraced, it seemed the stage had been set for the rest of my life.

When I turned three years old, my mom fell back into her old ways, getting caught up in a world of drugs, partying, and terrible relationships. That same year, her life tragically ended, leaving me motherless and my grandmother devastated.

My grandparents, despite their pain from having to bury their only daughter, stepped in and adopted me as their own. I started calling them Mom and Dad.

Because of adultery, however, it wasn't long before it was just Mom raising me. As an only child being raised by a single parent, I often felt like an outsider, as though I never quite fit in.

Mom, or Bebo as I'd often call her, likely influenced by the circumstances of her daughter's death as well as her husband's infidelity and the substance abuse that plagued our extended family, insisted on keeping me in private Christian schools until high school. She did all she could to shield me from the world, especially from boys. I'd often hear her stern warnings, even as a small child. "Your granddad snuck off to see Ann every chance he got," she'd say. "You better save yourself for a real good man, Nia."

The thought of someone cheating on me took root as a deep-seated fear in me. That's one reason I jumped at the opportunity to make Samuel Paul Rader my boyfriend less than a year after enrolling in public school.

He checked off all the standards that Bebo raised me to prioritize. He was a Christian. He didn't party. He didn't cuss. He didn't lie. He was a virgin. Sam quickly filled a gap in my life that I now recognize as the absence of a father, adoring me and loving me like a princess. Every time we had to say goodbye, the lost girl who didn't know her place in the world would resurface, and I'd count down the minutes until I could see him again.

Sam, who grew up without a father, also had some huge gaps he attempted to fill through our early relationship. The more time we spent with each other, the more intense our codependence became. Within the first month of our relationship, we were each other's everything.

****

As we sat inside the frozen yogurt shop, little paper cups and pink spoons in hand, Sam appeared to be trying to play it cool after the stranger in the parking lot recognized us. However, beneath the nonchalance, I could see that he was soaring.

He gazed off, staring through the window as he bit into his fro-yo as if he'd taken off to another world without us. The twinkle in his eye brought joy to my heart. I was desperate for Sam's emotional well-being, not only for his own sake but because it was crucial for me to receive the love and adoration I needed from him.

As we quietly finished our creamy treat, I grabbed my phone to catch up on the latest buzz surrounding our viral video. Our Facebook feeds continued to explode with more links to news articles about us, along with comments from friends we hadn't heard from in years. One person among them was our high-school theater teacher, the person who introduced Sam and me to lip-syncing.

"How crazy, Sam!" I shouted as a high school memory returned to me, "Remember when your lip-sync in high school basically went viral, too?!" Sam's performance for his theater class, a lip-sync to *I'm Gonna Be (500 Miles)* by The Proclaimers, was so well done that it was the only one, among many classes over several years, requested to be repeated before a larger audience.

"Oh yeah!" Sam said, turning his gaze from the window. "I guess it was a warm-up for this one."

Comments from viewers who were amazed by Sam's and my performance continued to pour in by the thousands. Some even accused us of being undercover talent for Disney. It seemed clear that something big was on the horizon, but all I could say for certain at the time was that I was elated for Sam and had hopes that it would revitalize his creativity and crazy personality and give me back the man I fell in love with.

3
Meet Cutie

An excellent wife who can find?
She is far more precious than jewels.
Proverbs 31:10

(Sam)

IT WAS MONDAY, March 10, 2014, at 6:41 PM, when I uploaded our lip-sync video to my inactive YouTube channel, *Samuel8955*, setting into motion an unimaginable life for our small family of four.

To add some friendly one-upmanship, I titled it *Good Looking Parents Sing Disney's Frozen, Love is an Open Door*. I'd admit that it was clickbait since we actually didn't sing, but considering the video would earn us the award for best video at the AMG Heritage Awards that year, I'd say it was more like clickart.

After making the video public, Nia and I wrapped each other in an embrace, savoring a moment of relief and accomplishment. It took us a week of fun and oftentimes frustrating practice together to get to our final take. With giggles and flirtatious touches, we exchanged a kiss, and I left for another night shift at the hospital.

The bond Nia and I developed, our shared creativity, and our determination while making the video meant more to me than a mere YouTube upload. The process brought us together, revealing things about our personalities that had attracted us to one another from the start, personality traits that we had allowed the stressors of parenthood and homeownership to push aside.

She sure is fun to get creative with, I thought as I drove to work.

I remembered making a similar lip-sync video with her in high school to the song *Collide* by Howie Day. I sang the chorus in my head, imagining her in the field of bluebonnets that I recorded her sitting in for the video: *Even the best fall down sometimes.* The words meant more to me than ever. I continued: *Out of the doubt that fills your mind, you finally find you and I collide.*

I pulled up the song in my iTunes library and played it loudly through the car speakers. I let my hand float and sway outside in the cool air outside my window, moving it to the strum of Howie Day's acoustic guitar. I joined in, singing, "The dawn is breaking, a light shining through…"

When the lyrics "You make a first impression" rang out, I fell silent. The line never failed to remind me of how intense my first impression of Nia was. The music faded into the background, and my thoughts drifted to the day I fell in love with her at first sight in our high school auditorium.

****

After another exhausting afternoon at work, building fences at a deer ranch to earn enough money to pay off the citations I had accumulated over summer break, I was dropped off at my high school where my twin brother, the lead in a play, was rehearsing.

Entering the dim auditorium where the rehearsal was taking place, I headed toward the only table occupied by students and not stacked chairs. As I approached it, indirect stage lighting revealed who was at the table: It was my sister Rachael, her friend Natalie, and my friend Scott. A fourth, unfamiliar face caught my attention—a cute girl. I woke up for cute girls. It was a welcome, unexpected surprise to my afternoon spent under the hot Texas sun.

I targeted the empty seat between Rachel and Scott, directly across from the intriguing brunette in a letterman jacket. Purposely scraping my chair loudly across the floor as I pulled it out from under the table, I succeeded in drawing her attention. Our eyes met for a split second, but at that moment, an undeniable spark flickered between us.

She's more than cute, I thought; *she's breathtaking.*

As I settled in my seat, my heart throbbed with a new rhythm, and judging by her subtle adjustments, I sensed that she also felt the sudden shift in the world. I was mesmerized and filled with questions. *Does she go to my school? Is she taken?* I hesitated to ask, fearing I already knew the answers.

The sudden realization that I needed to capture this girl's attention weighed on me. Normally, flirting was second nature, part of my daily high school routine. The closer I looked at her, however, the further out of my league she seemed and the more nervous I got about striking up a conversation with her.

I noted that all the previous years of flirting had merely been practice for this very moment. It was game day. I couldn't afford to be nervous.

Here we go, I thought. *It's time to sweep this girl off her feet.*

I swallowed hard and took a deep breath. *She's going to love this line,* I thought confidently. Then, I blurted it out. "You have big teeth," I said.

Her smile wavered between amusement and embarrassment. Rachael scolded me, "What the heck, Sam, shut up!"

Shoot! That sounded so much better in my head!

"And really big eyes," I added, trying to recover.

With a half smile, the beautiful girl replied, "Thanks?"

"Oh my gosh," Rachael said. "Sorry about my dumb brother."

"I mean that in a good way, obviously," I tried to explain. It didn't matter. I could have said "gobbledygook," and my intentions would still be unmistakable: I wanted her attention.

In another misguided attempt to impress, I propped my foot on the table, undid my Dr. Martin sandal straps, and scratched at a poison oak rash on my ankle. The table broke out in muffled laughter. Scott then pulled the sandal off my foot, and he and I began playing a game of tug-of-war with it until we were reprimanded from the stage.

"Be quiet!" The theater instructor hollered.

With my limited acting skills, I held onto my ankle, silently pretending my foot took on a rebellious mind of its own as I tried to wrestle the sandal back into place. Still looking down at her schoolwork, she smiled and shook her head. Then, I felt a tickle in my nose.

What the heck, I thought. *My nose is bleeding.*

With a pinch and a sheepish grin, I took off to the restroom.

Returning with an overly large wad of toilet paper stuffed in my nostril, the beautiful brunette said, "Aww," with an empathetic giggle. Whether she appreciated my vulnerability or was simply amused by my shamelessness, I was thankful to have her attention.

"So what's your name?" I asked.

"Nia," She replied.

"Do you go here?" I asked hesitantly.

"Yes," she replied.

I thought, *how on earth has this beauty been attending my high school and escaping my eyes?*

Although terrified, I asked, "Do you have a boyfriend?"

"Yeah," she laughed.

I grunted aloud like the sound a man makes when he walks into a brick wall. She laughed at me again.

"Who is he?" I muttered.

"He's in college," she said, "But who knows how much longer that'll last?"

Her response brought life back into my body. *Is she being sensitive to my feelings?* I wondered. She was far too special for a long-distance relationship. I would be her savior, her knight in shining armor. I mounted my horse and prepared for battle.

"Oh wow," I began. "It sounds like you need a new man." If there was one thing I knew I could offer a girl, it was romance and my full, undivided attention.

"Hah. Maybe," she replied, amused by my forwardness.

As the play rehearsal ended, the drama teacher called the production crew to the stage. Nia stood up gracefully, carefully slid her chair under the table then pivoted her petite body towards the stage.

This was my first time observing her full stature. As she strolled to the stage in her tight blue jeans, my breath shuttered, and my heart fluttered. *She's perfect,* I said to myself. *I've never seen true beauty till this night.*

I marveled at her luscious hair falling down her back as she attentively listened to the drama teacher debriefing the evening's rehearsal. I felt a sense of defeat as I watched her. I already belonged to her, but she belonged to someone else. Then, in a moment that seemed to suspend time itself, she began shifting her weight, opening herself up to me.

Will she turn to let me see her face? I thought. Then, with the grace and mercy of a dove, she did one better. She pushed her chin into her left shoulder and slowly slid her gaze toward me.

I perked up in my seat, smiling in anticipation of what I desperately wanted to happen next. *Let me see those big eyes*, I pleaded silently.

Then it happened.

An electrifying bond tethered us together as our eyes met and locked in place. The world seemed to stand still as God bestowed upon me the greatest gift of my life: Nia's attention. She parted her lips, unveiling the pearly whites that started it all. After I returned the smile, she turned back around.

Has my heart loved till now? I asked, taking the words straight from Romeo's mouth.

Sitting in the back seat of my mom's car, my forehead pushed against the damp window as I untangled the headphones for my iPod Mini, my twin brother called out from the front, "Did you talk to my girlfriend's friend tonight?"

"Who, Nia?" I asked.

"Yeah," he said.

"I definitely did!" I said, a smile beaming across my face.

"I knew you'd like her," he said, smiling back.

I fitted my earbuds into place, and as *The Scientist* by Coldplay started to play, I noted to myself that despite the darkness outside, the world appeared brighter and more vivid than it ever had.

Well, you're wrong, I thought in response to Michael's comment. *I love her.*

****

As I began my ER shift that evening, drawing up a dose of Ativan for my patient in alcohol withdrawal, I felt a deep longing to be with Nia. After administering the medication, I texted her in hopes of treating my own withdrawals.

"You look so gorgeous in our video," I wrote. "I really miss you."

"Thanks, Sammy! I miss you too!" came her quick response, followed by, "Guess what?"

"What?" I replied.

"All my friends on Facebook *love* the video!"

I texted back, "How could they not? You look amazing."

Sneaking a moment in the medication room, I checked Facebook on my iPhone 5. To my surprise, our video had garnered several shares. I began reading some of their posts:

You need to watch this! My friends just made the best video!

I can't believe these are my friends. Ah-mazing and hilarious!

WOW, I've watched this a hundred times! Must. Watch. Love you guys!

This couple is from my Church, and this is just great!

I noticed that our friends weren't sharing it merely out of support; it appeared they were taking personal pride in knowing the individuals on the screen, as if Nia and I were suddenly their celebrity friends.

What the heck is happening? I wondered.

An hour after getting home from work, when my colleagues and I saw our lip-sync on the Today show, an article was published by Today.com, titled, *Parents go viral with perfect "Frozen" lip-sync video.* It was official: we were going viral.

After speaking with several news outlets and believing our video had reached its peak, we received a game-changing email. It was Disney extending an invitation for a conversation.

A friendly voice came on the line, "Hello, this is Katherine from Disney. Am I speaking with Sam and Nia?"

We mostly remained silent on the call, absorbing more than we shared. Katherine and her colleagues showered us with praise for our unique spin on their iconic song. Just when we thought we couldn't be any more in awe, they asked us for a favor.

"Would you two possibly consider doing another video for us?" The voice of Disney inquired.

We probably could have negotiated to fulfill their request in exchange for a trip to Disneyland, some exclusive merchandise, or at least a percentage of the income generated from the video, but in our dizzying excitement, we eagerly blurted out, "Of course!"

Ten days later, our lip-sync rendition of *For the First Time in Forever* graced the internet. Disney's feedback was glowing: "This was absolutely awesome! Even better than the first one!" Katherine wrote.

Hearing such high praise from the world's leading entertainment company filled me with a kind of enthusiasm I had never experienced. Right then, I knew. Nia and I were about to embark on something special.

4
Pulling Curtains

I have said these things to you, that in me you may have peace. In the world you will have tribulation. But take heart; I have overcome the world.
John 16:33

(Nia)

VERSIONS OF OUR performance cropped up everywhere: firefighters belting it out in their firetrucks, police officers jamming in their cars, pilots singing mid-flight in their cockpits. Even the U.S. Naval Academy baseball team did a version of our *Frozen* lip-sync.

Our pastor and his wife, Bo and Chantel, threw a spontaneous gathering in their home to celebrate the success of our video. Given Bo's already extensive involvement in the YouTube space and Chantel's eagerness to love on others any chance she got, both were as thrilled about our video going viral as we were. It had only been two months since we started attending their church, a pivotal moment in our lives, and they were showering us with love and encouragement as if we were already family.

As the evening progressed and the other guests left, Sam and I stayed behind, seizing the opportunity to connect with Bo and Chantel and pick their brains about everything YouTube.

"So, what's the next move?" Bo asked.

"Well, right away," Sam began, "I saw this as an opportunity to share our faith."

"I saw that you mentioned our church in the description," Bo said. "I thought that was so cool."

"Yeah, totally," Sam said. "I definitely see this as a platform for me and Nia to keep doing that."

In the description of our video, Sam also included, "Our daily goal is to become more like Jesus."

"Oh, did we tell you guys the producers of the Ellen show interviewed us?!" I excitedly asked.

"What!? No way!?" Bo and Chantel said simultaneously.

"It didn't exactly work out, though," I said with a big laugh.

During our discussions with the producer at the Ellen Show, Sam and I candidly shared that we hoped to reflect Jesus for anyone seeing our video: a family of His making just enjoying life together. We figured that mentioning Jesus would likely ruin our opportunity to be on her show, so instead of staying silent, we voiced our beliefs loud and clear. The producers ended up offering the spot to a woman who copied our idea, doing a lip-sync to the same song in the front seat of her car with her daughter. She walked off the set with a $10,000 check. Sam and I called it a win.

"So what would it look like to make this into a Christian platform?" Bo asked.

"I think we would keep making lip-syncs and post them between family vlogs," Sam said, "and just show what it looks like for a family to live for Jesus."

"I like it, Sam," Bo said. "You guys will need a good end screen to get people subscribing. I'd be happy to make y'all one."

"That would be awesome!" Sam said, lighting up even brighter.

I watched on as Sam excitedly revealed his ideas for leveraging our viral video, hanging onto every piece of advice Bo had to offer. Watching Sam's creativity spark back to life was the highlight for me. I was so captivated by his enthusiasm that it was hard to concentrate on his actual words. I felt myself falling in love with him.

As the responsibilities of adulthood grew in our lives, Sam's stress grew even faster. He gradually lost interest in his passions, such as photography, woodworking, and music making, as if a part of himself was dying. Up until recently, beginning when we started a new church several months prior, he had been withdrawn, keeping his deeper thoughts and feelings from me, and I found myself walking on eggshells around him. His excitement that evening was a welcome sight.

When we first saw comments on our lip-sync video suggesting that we try vlogging, we were intrigued but clueless as to what it was. After a quick YouTube search, we stumbled upon families who were essentially sharing home videos with the public, adding their own commentary and bits of wisdom as they went along.

The comical thought of welcoming the entire world into our home led Sam and me to reminisce about one of our favorite memories: the first night we slept in our new home together.

****

Standing in the center of our soon-to-be bedroom, surrounded by emptiness, I was overwhelmed with excitement as Sam entered.

"Where does this go?" he asked, smacking a quick kiss on my nose. He held a box labeled "Wedding Gifts."

"Just wherever," I said.

Setting it down at our feet, he looked around, hands on his hips, and said, "This is it, cutie. Our own house. We can finally do whatever we want."

I giggled. "I know, right? Like, we can do *whatever* we want!"

"I kind of want to break a window just because I can, you know?" Sam joked.

"You better not!" I laughed. "Just that window probably took us a year to save up for!"

Intent on sleeping in the house on the first night, we unpacked the wad of blankets from our car and spread it out on the living room floor. We had received the keys to our new house the day before, but the electricity hadn't been turned on yet, and the sun was starting to set.

"Let's use the candles in the wedding box!" I shouted in excitement. Sam grabbed the candles and spread them throughout the living room.

As the sun finished setting, we settled together on the makeshift bed on the floor. The big living room window had no curtains, and our new house was in a tight suburban neighborhood. The flickering flame cast a warm glow, and we couldn't help but laugh about what our new neighbors across the street might've been thinking.

"We have nothing to hide," Sam said.

He stared up at the ugly track lighting suspended from the ceiling, his eyes shining as I rested my head on his outstretched arm. "After all these years dreaming of the day we'd never have to say goodbye," he said, "it's finally here."

"I know!" I said, trying not to get emotional.

Sam turned his head and locked his eyes on mine, staring deep into them in a way he always knew made me blush. "Stop falling in love with me," I said. Taking advantage of his romantic mood, I offered an idea. "I was thinking we could knock out that wall over there and open up the dining area," I said.

His stare turned into a sideways glance, "Maybe let me finish nursing school first?"

"Okay," I laughed. "At least remove this wallpaper."

"Why?" He asked, trying to conceal a smile. "You don't like the Beetlejuice look?"

I started tickling him. He screamed out, "Ahh, okay, okay! I'll do it!"

I sat up, threw my hands into my lap, and said, "So, we need to establish some ground rules."

"You're so cute," Sam said, "What's the first rule?"

"We've already decided that we're not having a TV in our room, right?" I asked.

"Yes," he said. "Maybe instead of watching TV, we can actually talk," He put *talk* in quotes with his fingers.

I giggled. "Well, either way, talking or *talking*, I think it's best."

He nodded, his focus surprisingly sharp as he looked at me. Having a particular look in his eyes, I braced for a romantic line to come out of his mouth. "Let's put a mirror on the ceiling instead," he said.

I started tickling him again, and our laughter echoed through the empty house. He wrapped me in a tight hug to lock up my arms, and I felt my heart swell. "I mean, maybe that would be fun," I said, playing along. As he freed me from his grip, I asked, "What other rules should we have?"

"We definitely can't ever use the word *divorce*," he reminded me.

"Never!" I exclaimed, "That was the last and only time it'll ever be said in this house!" I playfully demanded.

"You're adorable," Sam said. Blissfully unaware of the more important boundaries we were failing to make, we started kissing as if we had just figured out the key to a successful marriage. Then Sam whispered in my ear, "Time to break in the house."

****

"We can totally do this!" I said excitedly to Sam when he said vlogging sounded fun.

In one of our first family vlogs on the YouTube channel we rebranded as *Sam and Nia*, Sam uploaded a video titled *April Fools*

Prank on My Beautiful Wife. The video captures Sam making scrambled eggs for Symphony and then playing with our six-month-old son, Abram, just before lifting him from his crib to start the day.

Watching this vlog for the first time after Sam completed the edit, I fell deeply in love with the idea. If this vlogging journey meant we could immortalize moments of our babies' lives, then I was all in. That was when I pulled back our living room curtains, allowing the world to peer into our home. My favorite and most sacred place on earth became not just a living space but the studio and backdrop for our new public life.

5
First Class

God settles the solitary in a home; he leads out the prisoners to prosperity, but the rebellious dwell in a parched land.
Psalm 68:6

(Sam)

WHEN WE FIRST hit "upload," sharing our day-to-day lives with the world of YouTube, it was like detonating a dynamite of unthinkable opportunities. As our viewership and subscriber count skyrocketed, our inbox turned into a jackpot.

One of the first adventures that came our way was from none other than Disney. They decided we were cool enough to make several cameos in their official music video for their song *In Summer* from the movie *Frozen*. They flew our family to LA for a once-in-a-lifetime experience.

I played a bitter school bus driver, delivering a single but unforgettable line: "I guess you don't have much experience with heat." Nia transformed into the most beautiful lunch lady imaginable. Then, in another scene, Nia and I teamed up, playing the roles of geography teachers, enthusiastically delivering Olaf's iconic line, "Happy snowman!"

After returning home from one of the most exciting weeks of our lives, we soon received another shocking email. It was from YouTube, the actual company, offering to compensate us handsomely for yet another family trip to LA to play the leading roles in yet another music video.

With some seriously impressive makeup and prosthetics applied by the same artists who did Brad Pitt in *Benjamin Button*, they transformed us into the 70-year-old versions of ourselves. They had us lip-sync once again to *Love is an Open Door*, this time as if it were 40 years into the future and we were being admitted into a mental institution.

These crazy opportunities generated fun YouTube content, and the fun content, in turn, brought in even more opportunities. It was the best, seemingly never-ending cycle I could ever hope for. All I could do was thank the Lord and try to savor every moment. I attributed the success entirely to a prayer said over me just two months before our journey on YouTube began.

****

I sat with my arm around Nia in the pew of the small, nondenominational church we had started regularly attending two months earlier. "Jesus didn't come to call the guiltless, the equipped, or the righteous," Pastor Bo preached as he closed out his message, "He came to call sinners!"

I nervously fidgeted with Nia's shoulder as I listened to Bo use phrases such as "sowing the wind," "getting swept away by sin," and "reaping a whirlwind of emptiness." I was convinced God was speaking directly to me, and I couldn't sit still.

After years of exhausting every effort to escape my feelings of inadequacy without success, I came to a big realization that morning: I couldn't save myself from myself. An overwhelming desire welled up in me: I longed to walk with Jesus again.

"So if you've been following a path that has seemed right to you but has led you to a spiritual desert, as it inevitably will," Pastor Bo continued, "please head to the back and let someone from our team pray for you as we continue to worship."

A desert is the perfect way to describe where I am, I thought.

I had always avoided getting up for an altar call, believing at the time it was nothing but a public declaration of desperation. *I don't want people to think I can't handle life,* I'd say to myself. But this time, even though every nerve in my body screamed at me to remain seated, I got up. I squeezed past Nia, acutely aware and embarrassed that she was witnessing my admission of weakness.

I stepped into the middle aisle and made my way toward the back of the church, where a leader named Dan stood. "Hey, Sam," he said, taking a step closer. "How can I pray for you?"

My voice quivered with nervousness as I confessed to him how much I despised my job, my routines, and my constant sense of failure as a dad, a husband, and a man of God. I told him that I felt I wasn't making any difference in God's kingdom and that I was tired of feeling like I was merely meandering through life without any sense of purpose.

With a depth and intensity that hit me in my deepest parts, Dan said a warrior-like prayer over me. He declared life and rebuked self-deceptions, inviting God to remove hindrances that kept me from His assignment for my life. "You said the desert shall rejoice and blossom like a rose, Lord," Dan prayed. "Do that for Sam today. I declare it in the name of Jesus." He gave me a big hug after ending the prayer.

As I returned to my seat, discreetly drying my eyes with my shoulder, I knew something extraordinary had occurred. I felt an overwhelming sense of gratitude that God had not allowed me to remain seated. He gave a thirsty criminal, running through the desert, a cup of cold water, and I felt every drop coursing through my dehydrated body.

As Nia recalls, as we settled into our Honda Pilot to head home, she noticed a spark of hope return to my eyes. Indeed, that was precisely what I was experiencing for the first time in a long while: hope. Yet, as I leaned over the steering wheel, reflecting on Dan's prayer, sensing joy and purpose ahead, a stifling heaviness persisted.

Something was in my way. A burden. It was like I was a victorious soldier returning from war, having regained freedom but still sensing there was one more battle to fight before I could celebrate liberation. It nagged at me... like a small object in my shoe.

****

Eager to demonstrate my responsibility with the answered prayer, I immediately decided our channel would be a platform to share Jesus with the world, in turn fulfilling my prayers of desiring to be an active participant in God's kingdom.

Our outspoken faith didn't scare away subscribers like it seemed to have done with the producers of *The Ellen DeGeneres Show*. Our YouTube channel exploded. It quickly offered Nia and me an unprecedented level of financial stability through brand deals and

Google AdSense, bringing the dream of leaving a job I was unsatisfied with within reach.

Big corporations seemed eager to part with their money, handing us checks in the tens of thousands just for three-minute mentions of their product in one of our family vlogs. This windfall enabled us to do things we never considered possible. Previously, our tight budget meant declining even fast food outings, but with our newfound financial stability, we not only dined at upscale restaurants but also paid for others' meals and left $100 tips for our servers.

Our vacations, once limited to brief car trips, transformed into first-class flights to places all over the country. On one memorable occasion, we gave our first-class tickets to an elderly couple, which meant we took their seats in the back of the plane. This generosity, enabled by our unexpected wealth, became one of the most fulfilling aspects of the financial blessings that appeared to rain from the sky.

The income generated through YouTube didn't just cover wild adventures; it enabled us to pay off debts that had long hung over our heads: student loans, car loans, and even our mortgage. We were even able to help family members, easing some of their financial burdens as well. We weren't swimming in millions or stars in feature films, but we felt rich and famous, all the while proclaiming the name of Jesus at every opportunity.

Growing up, Nia and I knew all too well what it was like to live paycheck to paycheck, with our parents only ever purchasing what was absolutely necessary. I remember going days without running water or electricity while we waited for our mother to find a way to pay the bills. To say this new way of life was exciting for us would be an understatement. But as otherworldly as our new life became, the unexpected pitfalls hit us even harder.

6
CPS

*As for you, you meant evil against me, but God meant it
for good, to bring it about that many people
should be kept alive, as they are today.*
Genesis 50:20

(Nia)

IT WAS DECEMBER 31st, 2014. I sat on the cold hardwood floor of our living room, sculpting shapes out of Play-Doh with my toddler, Symphony, while nursing our infant, Abram.

"Should I vlog this?" I wondered, as I often did while doing my day-to-day activities.

Glimpses of scattered toys, shoes, and unfolded laundry in my living room served as reminders of my recent struggle with postpartum depression. Our home, which already appeared comfortably lived in, had become even more disorganized since Abram's birth. However, as the fog of depression began to lift from my mind over the previous month, I found myself ready to start decluttering.

I missed my old bubbly self and sensed its full return on the horizon. I was excited about getting back into my homemaking groove again when a knock at the door startled me out of my hopeful thinking.

I unlatched Abram and placed him on my hip. Wearing only my

robe, assuming it was a friend or family member, I opened the door and was met with the unfamiliar face of a middle-aged businesswoman with a clipboard. *Oh, great, I thought. What do they want me to buy today?*

"Hi," I said, trying to forgive this person for interrupting my and my baby's nursing time.

"Hello," the woman said with a bright smile. "My name is Tenille, and I'm with Child Protective Services. I have a few questions if that's alright."

I took a step back into the house. *Oh my gosh,* I thought, *whose children are in trouble?*

"Of course," I said. "Is everyone alright?"

"We've been informed by some of your online viewers of concerns that may be putting your children's safety at risk," the CPS agent said. "I'm here as protocol to follow up on those concerns."

"What?!" I shouted, leaning forward and clutching the pendant of the necklace Sam had gifted me just a week earlier on Christmas day.

****

After window shopping with my in-laws at a high-end mall, we returned to the exit doors where we had agreed to meet back up with our husbands. Once we arrived, we spotted our men inside Tiffany's, leaning over a counter and laughing boisterously.

We looked at each other with curious excitement. "Who's getting the little blue box under the tree this year?" I whispered. I was sure it wouldn't be me, so I directed my excitement at my sister-in-law, Rachel, who married Sam's brother, David. He and Rachel owned a successful cell phone business.

After sneaking up behind the boys, I pulled Sam aside and whispered, "Is Rachel getting Tiffany's for Christmas?"

"I guess so," he replied, "What a waste of money."

"Aww, that's so sweet, though," I said.

When Christmas morning arrived, with two children adding to the excitement, I hardly had time to consider what might be under the tree for me. In fact, I wasn't expecting anything. My gift was seeing Symphony's and Abram's joyous reactions to all the toys Sam and I had carefully picked out for them.

As the day came to a close, with our living room floor covered in wrapping paper, Sam reached for a small gift from behind the tree. My smile conveyed a gentle "You shouldn't have," yet inside, I was touched by his thoughtfulness and the extra effort he put into creating a surprise just for me.

As I began to peel back the layers of tape and paper, I caught a glimpse of the iconic Tiffany blue box and exclaimed, "No way!"

Sam laughed, "You're so cute."

"No, you didn't!" I shouted.

"I really did," he said.

"What is this, Samuel?" I demanded playfully, holding up the unopened box.

"Open it up and find out," he said, his eyebrows playfully bouncing up and down.

With my jaw dropped in awe, I opened the box and held up a shimmery silver necklace between Sam's face and mine. Dangling at the bottom of the chain was a key-shaped silver pendant with a sparkling diamond set in the center.

I gasped. "It's perfect!" I said.

"It's the key to my heart," Sam declared.

"What do you mean?" I asked, feeling loved as I turned to look him in the eyes

"You hold the key to my heart," he repeated, caressing my cheek. You always have and always will. I just want you to know that." I leaned in and kissed him, whispering my thanks between giving him another one. I turned around, allowing him to clasp the necklace around my neck, unaware of the deeper significance the moment held for Sam. I wouldn't know for another year, but he was silently recommitting himself to me.

****

"You're here about *my* kids?!" I shouted, instinctively snapping into fight or flight mode.

"Yes, ma'am," she replied. "It's protocol when we get a report of this nature."

My thoughts raced. *Are they going to take my babies!? Did we do something illegal!?*

More than any of my other abilities, I prided myself on being a good mother, always asking myself if I was raising my children the best way possible.

"Can I come inside?" Tenille asked.

"I guess," I said as I opened the door, my heart rate increasing. Of all days for someone to come into my home and judge me, that day was one of the worst. My house was a mess.

"Who called this in?" I asked. "What did they say? Did you even consider they might be lying?"

Opening up her clipboard, she pulled out a stapled packet. "The baby crib has chipping paint on it where your son has apparently been biting at the wood," she said, pointing at a screenshot from one of our vlogs. "Also, there was a trash can overflowing with diapers in his bedroom."

"That's why you came to see us?!" I replied, my voice rising in anger. "Of course, our trash can fills up with diapers!" Tenille stood nodding her head at me like she'd heard it a thousand times before. "Is it required by law to empty my trash by a certain time?!"

I soon regretted inviting this woman into our home. Caught up in the moment, I hadn't considered whether I had any other choice. While I've never been one to resort to physical violence, the urge to push her out of our house was almost too much to control.

"I'm sure there's nothing to be concerned about," she said, "but would you mind if I take a look around?"

While escorting her to Abram's nursery, she asked me about our YouTube channel. A flood of hateful comments we had received over the previous eight months flashed through my mind.

You're a horrible mother for feeding your kids that junk. You obviously don't know how to run a home. There was no shortage of people searching for flaws in my life.

After Tenille completed her walkthrough of our house, she sat down beside me on the loveseat in our living room. "May I ask your daughter a few questions?" she asked.

I nodded, desperate for the ordeal to end as quickly as possible.

As she started asking Symphony basic questions about herself, Sam walked in the door. Despite my request for him not to, he went straight for our camera and started filming.

"Babe," Sam began, "we have to show the haters that not even this will come between our family." He pointed the camera directly at Tenille and said, "You're fine, ma'am, go ahead."

After asking Symphony questions about her meals, sleeping conditions, and behaviors exhibited by her parents and brother, Tenille turned to a real bombshell that sent me boiling inside: "Do you know the parts of your body that are considered private?"

It took everything in me to keep quiet and not tell Tenille to leave our house immediately.

"Right here," Symphony responded, pointing at herself, clearly feeling uncomfortable.

Tenille continued, "Has anyone ever touched you there?"

Sam and I exchanged glances, shaking our heads in disgust and feeling a deep sense of violation. As Symphony innocently responded to her last question with, "No," a new wave of anger washed over me. The thought that someone had intentionally, and likely spitefully, put my child in this distressing situation infuriated me.

Get the ef out of my home! I screamed inside.

After 45 minutes of her unwelcome presence in our home, Tenille left, informing us that we would hear back from CPS in three days. The moment the front door latched closed, I crumbled into a puddle of angry tears in Sam's arms.

The following two days were painfully slow. I couldn't stop replaying the questions she asked, over-analyzing our answers and wondering if they were the right ones. Sam's confidence that the visit would amount to nothing, dismissing it almost as if it were a joke, only made the wait more challenging for me. On the third day, relief finally came.

We received an email confirming the case was closed, and no further action would be required. Although the experience was tortuous, it taught me a valuable lesson. I wasn't invincible to online haters like Sam seemed to be. I decided to do something about that.

After prayer and counsel, Tenille's visit ultimately contributed to my personal growth, making me a more resilient public figure. I began to understand that people weren't ridiculing me so much as they were trying to feel good about themselves. Their comments, whether negative or positive, said much more about them than they ever did me. I began to see value in criticisms, viewing hateful and judgmental comments as a chance to do what God does: take what the enemy meant for evil and turn it for good. Perhaps I did let the diapers pile up more than necessary. I could definitely appreciate that viewers are raising concerns about chipping paint on my child's bed.

Despite my initial response of wanting to share less online, I soon found myself wanting to share even more. With having CPS in my home and subjecting my baby girl to such personal questioning from a stranger, I believed I had faced the most daunting challenge there was to living in the public eye. If this couldn't break my spirit, then nothing could.

PART 2
Through the Wilderness
Weeks before full confession

7
Rings and Results

Therefore, a man shall leave his father and his mother and hold fast to his wife, and they shall become one flesh.
Genesis 2:24

(Sam)

IN MAY 2015, Nia and I made the conscious decision to discontinue the use of contraceptives, placing the timing of our third pregnancy squarely in God's hands. That's not to imply we regarded birth control as overpowering God's sovereignty; after all, our second child, Abram, was conceived while using protection. God operates on His own timetable; that much has been made *abundantly* clear in my life.

A year had passed since our first viral video, and I felt we were overdue for another hit. Given the proven success of pregnancy announcements on YouTube and Nia's and my decision to continue to grow our family, I felt the golden opportunity I was searching for was close at hand. My creativity was sparked. *How can we shock the world with our next pregnancy?* I wondered.

As an ER nurse, I administered numerous pregnancy tests, mostly for women requiring X-rays. While it's the doctor's responsibility to inform a patient of a positive result, I would rarely miss the opportunity to be present when a woman unexpectedly learned of her pregnancy.

"I'm pregnant!?" My patient questioned the doctor, her voice rising in disbelief. She had come to the ER expecting to hear she had another UTI, a familiar diagnosis. The doctor confirmed it and her mouth fell open as she turned to her mother sitting beside her. When the mother rose to her feet, her face absent of a smile, the doctor and I knew it was time to make our exit. Returning to my desk to document the dramatic interaction, inspiration struck.

Just like I knew my patient was pregnant before she and her mother did, I excitedly pondered, *could I somehow discover Nia's next pregnancy before she does?*

I Googled to check the originality of my idea and was beside myself to learn I was onto something groundbreaking. It had never been done before. Too excited to keep it to myself, I ran the idea by the ER doctor. He thought it was an interesting idea but commented, "That is if you don't mind stealing your wife's God-given right."

Later that night, I set aside a plastic urine hat used for collecting urine from patients, with the plan of discreetly placing it under the toilet seat at home to secretly obtain a sample from Nia. After realizing she'd likely notice the difference in the sound of urine hitting water and urine hitting plastic, I canceled the idea.

Plan B was to tickle her until she wet herself, then wring out the specimen onto a pregnancy test. *Probably not*, I admitted. *As if I can film that circus and get her okay to post it online.*

There was a simple solution; I just knew it.

Then, like a golden butterfly landing on the tip of my nose, the answer lit up my brain. Nia's habit of not flushing the toilet during the night was a running joke between us. She claimed it was to keep from waking everybody up, but I'd argue it was because she enjoyed seeing my reaction every morning to how much toilet paper she used.

At last, that first-morning sight of yellow water and TP has a silver lining.

That evening, after a brief nap, I sprang into action. As Nia prepared dinner, I turned off the water supply to our toilet and drained the bowl and tank. I then placed molding clay—yes, molding clay—in the back of the toilet drain to keep the urine specimen from going down when it came time for her to supply it.

"Hey, cutie," I said as we were getting ready for bed, biting my lip to keep from laughing, "the toilet's not working right now. It's okay if you pee in it, but please, no number twos."

"Umm, okay?" she laughed. I was sure she was onto me, but it turns out she never had a clue.

The next morning, voilà, an undiluted urine specimen awaited me at the bottom of the toilet. I grabbed our vlogging camera, snuck my way into the bathroom, and explained to the camera what I had done. Using a dropper, I siphoned up a few drops of her pee and squeezed it onto the pregnancy test. After waiting a minute, the results were revealed... *Negative.*

I deleted the footage from the camera, removed my clay dam, and turned the water back on. "Fixed it!" I announced from the bathroom.

Two weeks later, I repeated the process, getting yet another negative result. By the third try, I ditched the clay dam and wasn't even bothering to drain the toilet anymore. My enthusiasm for the idea was waning. Three weeks later, while at work, ready to throw in the towel, Nia texted, "I'm late on my period."

"You better not do a pregnancy test without me!" I quickly texted back. *It's now or never.*

I got home at 8 AM, just as Nia was whisking eggs for breakfast. After kissing her and the kids, I announced, "Time to take the Browns to the Super Bowl," then beelined it to the bathroom. I peered into the toilet, spotting the golden liquid I was there to collect, along with half a roll of toilet paper. For the fourth time, I siphoned up her pee water, pushed three drops onto the pregnancy test, and waited for the results as the camera, once again, watched on. The result appeared fast, nearly knocking me off my feet. "Oh my gosh!" I exclaimed, my hand covering my mouth as I tried not to spoil the surprise. "She's pregnant!?"

Although I thought I was prepared for the test to one day come back positive, my immediate reaction proved otherwise. I was so focused on executing my plan that the realization that Nia and I could actually be expecting another child had completely slipped my mind. My children had always been the greatest joys of my life, and suddenly, I found myself learning we'd be blessed with another one. I was elated by the news that in nine months, we would have another baby in the house.

There had only been one other instance in my life when an eagerly awaited moment, one I was fully aware was coming, blindsided me as unexpectedly as that positive pregnancy result did. Nothing in the world could have ever prepared me for it. It was on my wedding day.

****

I stood at the altar under a towering oak tree, my body tense with nerves. Our pastor, Brother Tim Mabe, sensed my unease. "Everything is going to be great, Sam," he assured me.

Waiting for Nia to emerge from her aunt and uncle's front door and begin her walk through their front yard toward me, my eyes shifted to the DJ, who was struggling to play the music on cue.

What's taking him so long, I anxiously thought.

Inspired by my favorite scene in the first movie of the trilogy, *Back to the Future*, I had chosen *Earth Angel (Will You Be Mine)* by The Penguins for the song Nia would walk down the aisle to. Nia had wanted *Lucky* by Jason Mraz as the song, but that morning, as we prepared for the day, I found myself pleading with her to walk down the aisle to this old favorite of mine instead. In high school, the song sparked my exploration of romance and led me to a lifelong hobby of writing love songs of my own. It represented the dream of one day meeting a girl who embodied all it meant to me. Nia had become that girl. Although she wasn't particularly fond of the song initially, she'd later agree it was the perfect choice.

The song started playing, "Earth angel, earth angel, will you be mine…"

I turned my attention from the DJ to the end of the aisle, and before my eyes could adjust, I sensed a holy beauty beaming in my direction. Something was physically there, but in its initial presence, I struggled to comprehend what it was. It was like the heavens opened up before me, offering me a glimpse inside, but my earthly flesh was too simple to grasp it. The spiritual encounter brought me to tears as my eyes finally caught up with my heart.

It was Nia… in a wedding dress… my bride… as if she had teleported straight from the day I fell in love with her, her full beauty tantalizingly shrouded behind a thin wedding veil. Her eyes sparkled with innocence, and her smile, radiant and sincere, turned me back into the lovestruck teenager who had been completely enamored by the first sight of her five years earlier.

Despite being fully aware of the coming moment, the sight of Nia in white took me by total surprise. Apparently, I had underestimated how much my soul yearned to see the love of my life in a wedding gown. The world around me disappeared, and all I could see was her.

The song continued: "I'm just a fool… a fool in love with you." As far as I was concerned, this was the climax of not just our relationship but of my entire life. My tears started to flow even harder. I swiped at my eyes, desperate not to miss a single second of her willingly approaching me, ready to spend the rest of her life with me. I couldn't believe that such an angel had chosen me.

After her father placed her hand in mine, I gently pulled her in close, fighting the intense urge to kiss her before instructed. "I love you so much," I whispered through sniffles.

"I love *you*," Nia said, a tear rolling down her cheek.

As Brother Tim began his opening prayer, I felt a trickle from my nose. Signaling my twin brother Michael, my best man, for a tissue, I dabbed at it and discovered I was having a nosebleed. I frantically rolled up a piece of the tissue and stuffed it into my nostril, hoping the prayer would last long enough for it to stop bleeding. As everyone else had their heads bowed in prayer, I couldn't help but think how oddly coincidental my situation was.

The first day I met Nia was also marked by a nosebleed. An abrupt and uncontrollable nosebleed felt like an interesting parallel for love at first sight that seemed to be happening all over again. Was the universe drawing a full circle? I realized these weren't ordinary nosebleeds; they were symbols of how deeply Nia affected me. I later thought how fitting it was that blood was shed on the day I made my covenant to my bride.

Taking a deep breath, I unfolded a paper from my pocket and began to read the vows I had written her: "Before God and everyone else, I declare my love to you and promise to stand by you forever." Her eyes glistened as I continued: "I promise to never give up on us, to be true to you, to love you in good times and in bad, and to honor you all the days of my life."

Nia slid my wedding band onto my finger, rightfully assuming it would never be removed. At that moment, she made our motto, the one we had etched on the inside of my wedding band, official. We would always be...

A team hard to beat.

"Sam," Brother Tim said, looking at me and pausing with a big smile, "you may kiss your bride."

I lifted Nia's wedding veil, revealing the big, beaming eyes and teeth that started it all. As if not wanting to waste a single drop, I cradled her face and kissed her. After five years, we were finally one.

"I now present to you, Mr. and Mrs. Samuel Rader!" Pastor Mabe announced. The audience rose to their feet and cheered as Nia and I walked hand in hand into our new lives, eager to embrace the unknown together.

****

"Okay, what should I do?" I whispered into the camera. "How am I going to announce it?"

I knew I wanted to prolong the moment of telling Nia she was pregnant for as long as possible, but I wondered how I would keep it interesting and entertaining between now and then. Hoping for the best, too excited to think, I slipped the pregnancy test into my chest pocket and decided I'd improvise.

As I walked from the bathroom to the kitchen, a realization dawned on me: this pregnancy would likely be our last. Considering Nia's history with two prior C-sections, our doctor warned us that the risks of a fourth child were too great and that three pregnancies would be our max.

I thanked God for the blessing of another addition to our family, yet the realization that this moment would be the last time we'd share the unique joy of learning a new baby was on the way was sobering. It was a bittersweet reminder of the passage of time, a moment between chapters of our lives that, once crossed, could never be revisited. Even still, the moment carried more weight than I could have ever imagined.

8
Muffled Joy

*Why are you cast down, O my soul, and why are you
in turmoil within me?*
Psalm 42:11

(Nia)

BETWEEN FILLING SIPPY CUPS, draining bacon grease, and wiping down countertops, I turned around to see Sam entering the kitchen from our bedroom, holding our camera and recording. We vlogged every day, capturing moments at all hours, but something about his smile told me he was up to no good this time.

"What are you doing?" I asked as he followed me around the kitchen. I wondered if I was supposed to know something but had forgotten it. Then, suddenly, he made an out-there kind of joke as I reached for the jelly in the pantry.

"Is that wine?" he asked. "Oh yeah, you can't have wine."

Before I could so much as call him a dummy, he followed it up with, "Why don't you have a bologna sandwich? Oh yeah, because you can't have bologna."

I shook my head as I realized what he was trying to suggest. "Guys, *he's* the one full of baloney," I said, looking into the camera. "He doesn't know *what* he's talking about."

I assured Sam that I wasn't pregnant, feeling sure my period was going to start in the next couple of days. I asked him to please stop filming and end his crazy antics. I had no idea what he was up to. Still, I definitely did not want to play around about a pregnancy that I was confident I did not have, especially given how complicated and emotional each of my other pregnancies had been.

****

It was September 18th, 2013, at 5 AM, six months before our YouTube debut, when I went into labor with our second child. Given that Symphony was born via an emergency C-section three years prior, coupled with my plans to have a vaginal birth, my delivery was deemed high-risk.

By 1 PM, despite my intense pain, my labor had not progressed. The doctor ordered a C-section, and within the hour, I was cradling my chubby, handsome, snuggly boy, Abram Samuel Rader. I'll never forget how he took to nursing like a champ from the start. My heart expanded, and the love I could give as a mother doubled in capacity. I was utterly smitten by my tiny guy and never wanted to put him down. However, after a week of pure bliss with our new baby, my world started rotating differently.

A thick haze came down over my thoughts. It felt like I was stuck in a bad dream, watching my life but not really living it. Week after week, days and nights blurred into one another, turning my life into a seemingly endless, dreary cycle.

I couldn't make sense of the sadness. The months following having my first child, Symphony, were the exact opposite. She brought new colors into my life, turning the deep love that Sam and I had for each other into something tangible and visual.

My doctor soon diagnosed me with postpartum depression.

I remained in the thick of it for many months. To make matters worse, Sam was also struggling with depression. Gradually, our home shifted from being stable and routine-oriented to disorganized and emotionally unpredictable.

I gazed at the chore calendar I had created the week before my delivery. The sight of it pushed me even deeper into depression. I had laid out a schedule for house duties, hoping it would help me stay on top of them once Abram arrived, but I could never even attempt it. I barely recognized the person I had become.

One night, after putting the children to bed, I approached my washing machine, intent on washing a load of clothes. All I could do was stare at it. I felt hopeless in focusing my attention on anything other than the unique sadness that had seemingly taken complete ownership of me. For the first time, the simple task of doing laundry seemed impossible.

As I stood there in a daze, I began wondering how Sam dealt with his depression, which had been a recurring issue for him since I had known him. I was aware that when he had a hands-on project, it helped, but as of late, he hadn't been building anything.

What is Sam putting all his creative energy into? I wondered.

I realized that the last project he had worked on was over a year ago, when he restored an old toy box for Symphony. He liked to sleep. But what about when he was at work? Sleep was obviously not an option there. As I spiraled down a depressive rabbit hole concerning Sam, I became convinced that there were hidden layers to his struggle he was either unwilling or perhaps unable to share with me.

Surrounded by untouched piles of laundry, dirty dishes, and unanswered questions, the weight of my depression grew heavier. I dragged myself to bed and fell into a restless sleep.

****

After believing Sam had gone back to our bedroom to put our camera away, he returned not only with the camera but with even more ridiculous statements. In an exchange that didn't make it into the final video, I said, "Cutie, just stop. Sit down and eat. I'm too tired for all this."

He replied, "Cutie, please. I have an idea here."

After I agreed to let him proceed with whatever he was trying to pull, certain none would make it on our channel, he told me to reach into his chest pocket. After pulling out the surprise, I was so puzzled and embarrassed for Sam that I could only laugh. It was a used pregnancy test showing a positive result.

Through my laughter, I said, "You're such a dork!" and nearly fell out of my chair. Sometimes, or many times, Sam finds humor in things I see none in, but this one took the cake. The idea that he took home someone else's used pregnancy test from the hospital was so wacky that it was both hilarious and concerning.

"It's true," he said, looking into my eyes.

At five years old, Symphony responded as I rolled my eyes, "You're pregnant, Daddy?"

I looked into the camera held in Sam's hand and assured our viewers that I was *not* pregnant. "This. Is. A. Joke," I said as I clapped my hands on each beat.

"Yeah, it is a joke," Sam said, turning the camera to himself. "The joke's on you."

Once the laughter and wildness faded from his eyes, the kitchen grew quiet, giving me a moment to gather my thoughts. *Wait, I thought, he's actually scheming something serious here.* Then, when I noticed a depth enter his eyes, it hit me.

My body went into a unique and confused state of shock. "What did you do?!" I exclaimed, "Did you get a dropper out of the toilet?!" The words came out before I could even process what I was saying.

"I did," Sam responded, misty-eyed. At that moment, I understood what he had done.

"No way!?" I said, trying not to burst into tears. "Are you serious right now!?"

Symphony, watching all the commotion unfold, looked up at me and confusingly asked, "You're pregnant?"

After a whole year of trying, I was finally pregnant, and my husband was the person to deliver the news. I couldn't believe it. I became a ball of emotion, not knowing which way to roll. After taking another pregnancy test and confirming that what Sam claimed was true, I let the joy of knowing there was a new life in my womb overwhelm me. It was the most intense moment of my life… up to that point.

9
Viral Again

*The Lord waits to be gracious to you, and, therefore
He exalts himself to show mercy to you.*
Isaiah 30:18

(Sam)

ONCE OUR PREGNANCY announcement video finished uploading to YouTube at noon, the day after filming it, the familiar names of our loyal subscribers flooded the comment section.

"Heartfelt congratulations!" a comment read.

"We're over the moon for you!" read another.

The views immediately skyrocketed. But it wasn't just being watched; it was being felt. On Facebook, tags and shares multiplied as friends, family, and beyond exclaimed how the video was a bright spot in their day and how it evoked tears of joy.

"I haven't cried like this in ages," a stranger wrote.

By 5 PM, amidst the non-stop pings of our phones, Nia and I exchanged a wide-eyed glance.

"I think it's happening again," I said.

"Hehe," Nia laughed. "This is nuts."

As we sat down for dinner at the house of our friends and mentors, Heath and Amanda, a message from a college friend popped up in my notifications. "You made it to Fox13now.com!" He wrote. Sure enough, there we were, our faces lit up with the joy of a new pregnancy featured on a major news platform. We were officially, for the second time, going viral.

After refreshing the view count and reading through comments for the umpteenth time, I turned off my phone and sank into thought as I bit into a brownie. Trying to articulate to myself the unique emotion I was experiencing, I settled on a single word: chosen.

Is God still not done answering my prayer? I wondered. *What does this mean, God?*

Given my inclination toward self-glory and finding personal value in who and how many people took notice of me, I asked Heath to say a prayer of guidance for me on handling the flood of attention. The last thing I wanted was for what I knew would be a fleeting moment to push my relationship with the Lord to the back burner, as my tendency was when life started to go well for me.

This is the best pregnancy announcement ever! I distractedly recalled reading in the comment section as Heath said his prayer. *Your idea was sheer brilliance!*

As I fought the urge to praise myself and wallow in the high of widespread validation, my mind turned to a seemingly prophetic childhood memory that held more significance than ever.

"Just grant him wisdom to navigate this new season with grace and humility. Amen," Heath prayed.

As we pulled out of Heath's driveway and headed for my mom's place, I shared the memory with Nia.

****

When I was eleven years old, on a routine trip to our local grocery store, my mother, with all six of her children in tow, stood at the checkout, sifting through her purse for coupons and her food stamps card.

The grocery bagger, a tall, middle-aged man with a curious look on his face, was filling our bags with marked-down Cornflakes and cat food when he asked Mom a common question.

"How many kids you have?" he asked.

"Six," Mom replied as she laid a stack of coupons on the counter.

The bagger's eyebrows shot up. "Wow, you have your hands full," he said.

Mom's silent response conveyed she'd heard his comment too many times before.

Upon loading the last bag into the cart, I watched a spark of inspiration hit him. As he looked down at me, meeting my eyes, he said with a crooked smile, "With such a big family, that increases the odds one-uh y'all will be famous." He laughed.

It was an offhand comment, one I had never heard or thought about, a joke unrelated to anything that day, but it struck a chord with me. The comment lingered with me for many years, to the extent that by my sophomore year of high school, I was 100% convinced that fame was in my future.

I wrote in my journal, "Today, I can barely hold back my smile because certain events happened today that indicate I'll for sure be famous one day."

****

I looked at Nia, shaking my head in disbelief. "Can you believe this is happening *again*?" I asked.

The idea that my immature high school dream of fame, which I didn't achieve then on account of having no real talent or grit, was being realized once more simply on account of a silly family home video was mind-boggling. Maybe I was falling into my usual pattern of overanalyzing, but I kept wondering, *why is this happening to us again?*

"I've wanted this too bad for it to happen a second time," I admitted.

As Nia maintained my gaze, her eyes reflecting the same uncertainty as mine, it became evident that we both sensed something suspicious about our rare situation. The question that hung in the dark evening between us that neither of us could put into words was about the unseen strings that were likely attached.

By the time we arrived at my mom's apartment, our video had climbed to the number one spot on Facebook's trending list, edging out Rosie O'Donnell's response to Trump's comments in the Republican debate. Big names like People Magazine, E! Online, Fox4News, Insider, and pretty much every other major outlet were talking about it. We would even land a spot on the Today show for the second time in our lives the following morning.

I couldn't help but laugh as I imagined the dilemma the producers of *The Ellen DeGeneres Show* likely found themselves in. I pictured them deliberating: "Should we have Sam and Nia on *this* time or wait till a different husband pulls this off?"

I tapped open an article a friend sent our way. The author, Sammy Nickalls, in her blog on *Hellogiggles.com*, wrote of the reasons why she believed the video caught on like wildfire:

> *We've seen our fair share of super adorbs pregnancy announcements… we thought we had seen it all. But oh boy, were we wrong. A recent vid by Youtube vlogging couple and high school sweethearts Sam and Nia has been going totally viral, and for good reason: it's not only one-of-a-kind, but a serious tearjerker. So he tested a sample of urine she left in the bathroom. . . only to discover that it was positive. And Sam's response is ADORABLE. Of course, the sample was diluted from toilet water, so the couple did another test to be sure, but turns out that Nia is absolutely pregnant!*

By the end of the third day, after a reporter from the Dallas Morning News knocked on our front door to request an interview, nearly 10 million people had viewed our pregnancy announcement. What started as a crazy idea and a willingness to meddle with my wife's urine morphed into a global celebration of sorts.

Our babysitter was excited when she texted us that she had heard total strangers talking about our video in line at a Nike store. She couldn't resist telling them, "Guess what? I'm their babysitter!"

Days later, a large picture of our family would make the front page of our local newspaper, the Terrell Tribune. Before that day, however, just as we were grasping the enormity of our video's influence, celebrating the exciting moment with my mom, our lives took a shocking and painful turn.

10
Handful of Tears

*Hope deferred makes the heart sick,
but a desire fulfilled is a tree of life.*
Proverbs 13:12

(Nia)

AS OUR FAMILY JOYFULLY climbed the stairs to Sharon's apartment—Sam's mom—a twinge of discomfort in my lower abdomen caught me off guard. Once inside, while Symphony and Abram dashed towards the play area and Sam towards the couch, I headed to the restroom, hoping to alleviate the discomfort.

After sitting on the toilet, I noticed a faint spot of blood in my underwear. *That's strange,* I thought.

Attempting to brush it off as nothing serious, I exited the restroom and joined Sam and his mom on the couch, watching our pregnancy announcement video on the living room TV.

"How many views now?" Sharon asked, thrilled about another grandchild and proud it was making headlines.

"Almost 600 thousand," Sam said.

"Wow!" she said, "I told you you were special." I chuckled. It always bothered Sam when his mom bragged about him. "Nia, I can't tell you how happy I am for you," she added. "Are you excited?"

"I'm *so* excited," I said, trying to suppress the thought that I was possibly still bleeding.

As Sharon began asking Sam about how he got the idea for the video, I pulled out my phone as a distraction and opened up the comment section on our video.

"Here comes the haters," I said after reading the most recent comments.

"That just means it's reaching a bigger audience," Sam said.

Viewers were beginning to accuse us of staging the video, claiming that it was impossible to get an accurate pregnancy result from a diluted urine sample. I couldn't help but respond to one of them. "I guess you didn't watch until the end of the video," I wrote. "I did a second test to confirm it."

A cramp in my lower abdomen caught me off guard again. I couldn't ignore it. "I'll be right back," I quietly said as I headed back to the restroom.

I was met with a fresh, even larger amount of blood in my underwear. My heart sank as the reality of what was possibly happening began to sink in. *I've never had this happen before,* I thought. *Could this really be what I think it is?* A wave of fear came over me, adding a whole other discomfort to my stomach.

How am I going to tell Sam and Sharon? I thought as I exited the restroom.

As I rounded the corner into the living room, tears clouding my vision and my heart pounding painfully fast, I prepared to deliver news that horrified me. "Guys?" I began, suddenly hating being the one to spoil such a joyous moment. As soon as Sam and Sharon made eye contact with me, I covered my face with my hands and broke down in tears. "I'm bleeding."

"Oh no, cutie," Sam said as he rushed to me. He wrapped me in a hug and reminded me that I had experienced spotting in my first pregnancy, and everything turned out great. "A little bit of spotting can be normal," he said.

"It's different this time," I whispered. "Something's wrong."

"Oh no, sweetie," Sharon said, "Let's start praying."

We sat down, and after Sam said a prayer, he started crying, followed by his mom.

As our emotions slowed, Sam picked up our vlogging camera, "Hey guys, some sad news here," he said into the lens. "Nia just found out she's starting to spot a little bit, and she's having some cramping. We're pretty upset about it."

"If no cramps were attached to it," I added, "it would be different, but it just feels weird. I've never felt this in pregnancy."

We didn't have much else to say. Sam shut the camera off after one last message. "We'll keep you guys updated." That footage never made it into a vlog.

"I feel so confused," Sam mumbled. "How could we go from such a high to such a low so quickly?" I felt the same way. It was as if a thief had entered the apartment and yanked the joy right out of our hands before we could even realize what happened.

After ten minutes of listening to our kids happily play in the next room, we said goodbye to Sharon and made the sad stairwell descent back to our car, the joys of a new life and a runaway success overshadowed by fears of a miscarriage.

I entered our car slowly and carefully, as if I could keep the baby safer that way. The drive home was gloomy, quite different from our spirited drive there. As we pulled into the driveway of our painted blue brick home, I broke the silence with more gut-wrenching news.

"Oh no, I just felt something drop!" I frantically exclaimed.

"Oh no, cutie," Sam replied with pain in his voice.

I hurried into the house and locked myself in the hallway bathroom. I sat on the toilet with my face in my hands and realized that the discomfort I felt at Sharon's place was the beginning of my baby being pulled from my body's grip.

"Don't let go, baby," I begged.

I sat on the toilet, terrified of what would happen next. My baby, too fragile, couldn't hold on any longer. Before I could fully prepare my heart for it, a small mass dropped out of me, making a tiny splash as it broke the surface of the water. It would be the only sound I'd ever hear from my unborn baby.

I wailed a guttural scream the instant I felt her leave, desperately wanting to go back in time and do everything possible to prevent the moment from continuing. The sounds that escaped my mouth were unnerving, even to me. My grief was so raw and deep that I couldn't even begin to suppress it. My insides were crying out as if my very soul was hurting. I wanted my voice to carry the pain as far away from me as possible, but the wailing only intensified it.

Feeling tears filling my hands, I knew I had to move. I stood up and, without glancing down, ran to our bedroom where Sam was and fell into his lap and cried even harder. As he wrapped me up, he realized the miscarriage was final and began crying with me. All we could do was wait for the massive wave of grief to pass over us as we tried to comfort each other.

Fifteen minutes must have passed before I finally looked up at him and said, "There's no way we can just flush it down! That's our baby in there!"

Sam mustered the strength to get up. The sound of the bathdoor opening was quickly followed by deeper cries from him. The pain in his voice was unlike anything I had heard from him before. Suddenly, my heart ached even more, not just for our loss but for Sam's pain as well.

So sweetly and so gently, like the amazing father he was and is, Sam scooped up the embryo and placed it in a Ziploc bag. The following morning, we visited a garden center as a hurting family of four. We chose a potted angel plant, took it home, and made its soil the final resting place for our lost baby.

That day marked a huge shift for both of us. In a way, we had a growth spurt together. Death, hitting home for the first time, changed our reality and forced us to see life's frailty like never before. Just as I began to adapt to this new perspective as a mother, I unknowingly stood on the verge of another life-altering experience.

The distress of having a miscarriage, the abrupt end to the excitement of our pregnancy announcement, and the uncertainty of what it all held for our near future left us in silent confusion and worry. I went to bed that night, praying that our lives would go back to normal as soon as possible.

PART 3
Burned, Not Consumed
Days before full confession

11
Rumored Remorse

*My son, do not despise the Lord's discipline or be weary
of his reproof, for the Lord reproves him whom he loves,
as a father the son in whom he delights.*
Proverbs 3:11-12

(Sam)

NIA AND I SAT side by side in dining room chairs in our family playroom, studio lights and ABC news cameras focused on our faces.

"Some skeptics say it was just a ploy to get more followers—that you staged the whole thing," stated the ABC reporter, Aditi Roy, referring to our pregnancy and miscarriage YouTube uploads. "How do you respond to that?"

Two weeks prior, Nia and I announced our miscarriage to our YouTube audience in a video we titled Our Baby Had a Heartbeat. Immediately upon upload, we were met with an unpredictable negative reaction. Many viewers found it unbelievable that we had a miscarriage so soon after posting such a remarkable pregnancy announcement, accusing us of fabricating everything and reinforcing earlier claims that testing diluted urine for HCG hormone wasn't possible. According to them, this meant that since we had to get out from under the faked pregnancy, we had to fake a miscarriage.

I answered Aditi's question with honest conviction. "Especially as Christians, we would never deceive our audience like that," I said. It was true. We hadn't faked anything regarding our pregnancy and miscarriage, but if I had been aware of the greater trials ahead, I might have been more cautious in my response.

The ugly reality was, as I would prove in the coming days, that even as a Christian, I was capable of—even willing to—deceive our audience if it meant saving face. The ABC interview we gave that day was scheduled to air on Nightline a few days later, ironically just one day before I would blatantly lie to our audience about an entirely different matter.

The day after our ABC interview, Nia noted that I was "particularly tense" as we made our way to DFW airport, bound for Seattle to attend VloggerFair—a gathering of like-minded video creators. As if the miscarriage itself wasn't enough, the hate and doubt surrounding our videos drove another huge wedge between my excitement of going viral and our future as YouTubers. My hit video had dissolved into a muddled drama.

Just as our first viral video, the *Frozen* lip-sync, sparked a trend on YouTube, so too did our miscarriage announcement. This time, however, the trend thrived on making us the laughingstock of the internet. Famous YouTubers, newer creators, and everyone in between began making parody videos mocking both my act of testing Nia's urine as well as Nia's emotional public response to our miscarriage, where she allowed her tears to run freely. Even the ones who believed our story found our situation worthy of being mocked. Previous thoughts of feeling like a genius turned into doubts that I was even a sane person.

As if our vulnerable YouTube uploads didn't give the crowds enough to jeer at, in bad judgment, but an innocent attempt to find meaning in our suffering, I tweeted: "Our tiny baby brought 10M views to her video and 100k new people into our lives." Because of the tweet, we were then accused of openly bragging about the profit that the loss of our baby brought us.

I'd soon admit that drawing a connection between views and a pregnancy that ended in miscarriage was indeed imprudent. However, I was mistaken in believing that those who mattered to us would understand my intentions were only good. Expecting fellow family vloggers to extend grace during such a difficult time proved to be overly optimistic.

"This is messed up," a YouTube creator in the family vlogging space tweeted in response to mine.

His response felt like a betrayal, particularly for Nia, and especially when another family she had been eager to meet "liked" the condemning tweet. Seeing Nia's disappointment pushed me over the edge.

How am I going to deal with this one, I wondered. I began regretting turning down the PR manager who had offered his services to us when our story first broke.

Other tweeters used words like "disturbing" and "super gross" to describe my tweet. Some even suggested I needed help. Heeding the wisdom of one response—"Views and likes are not life. Take some time to heal with your real family and friends."—I removed the Twitter app from my phone, admitting that I wasn't in the right state of mind to make any more public statements.

My controversial tweet unintentionally exposed an ugly truth about myself, a flaw of which I was already well aware. Views, likes, and subscriber counts had become deeply intertwined with who I had become. My mentor, Heath, often prayed for me: "God, let Sam know that his identity is not dependent upon how many thousands of views he may or may not get but upon Your performance 2,000 years ago on the cross."

Ten years before Nia and I gained popularity on YouTube, I made a journal entry predicting that I would be ensnared by my future "celebrity status." I wrote, "On the way home from school today (on the bus), I saw a kite stuck in a tree and wondered if that's how I will be. I'll get to the top, and I'll be stuck there." I concluded, "If I have God in my life, that's impossible, so whatever."

I was, indeed, stuck and needed God to get me out. Yet it would still come as an unexpected surprise when He would soon do just that.

We faced criticism from every direction, so Nia was right: I was "particularly tense" as we headed to the airport for our flight to Seattle that evening. Despite the overwhelming situation—navigating miscarriage emotions, responding Christ-like to news outlets and commenters about false rumors, dealing with unexpected criticism from those we thought had our backs, sympathizing with a hurting wife, and stressing about the Nightline interview release—beneath it all, my biggest concern was something else entirely that was circulating the internet, something that had the potential of annihilating everything I ever truly loved.

(Nia)

On August 20th, 2015, immediately after my dentist had corrected a botched cavity filling from the day before, I returned home to an anxious Sam. Even though our flight wasn't due to depart for another five hours, we said our goodbyes to the kids and set off for the airport.

We were headed to our first YouTube event as *featured* creators. I was thrilled we would be recognized alongside some of the platform's most popular vloggers, such as ItsJudysLife, The Shaytards, and the Daily Bumps. Sam usually loved to travel and appreciated new experiences, but this time, his enthusiasm was nowhere to be seen.

"What's wrong?" I asked. "Please don't be upset. I want to have a good time with you."

Sam replied, "This whole vloggerFair thing is so dumb."

I was fully aware of his anger regarding a tweet from a fellow YouTube vlogger—I was still upset myself—but I sensed something else was going on.

"Just tell me," I said. "If it's the tweet, let's not let it ruin our trip."

Sam was irritable, and our exchange quickly got heated. As we approached a highway bridge, the kind I had always been terrified of driving over, fear came over me. "Slow down, Sam!" I demanded. Sam laughed as he explained he was going 10 under the speed limit.

"These bridges make me nervous too, cutie," Sam said.

Our tense conversation abruptly ended.

Upon arriving at the airport, Sam was so engrossed in his phone that I found myself leading us to our gate for the first time in the history of our relationship. It was a sign of things to come, hinting at significant changes ahead.

12
Ashley Madison

But if you will not do so, behold, you have sinned against the Lord, and be sure your sin will find you out.
Numbers 32:23

(Sam)

"THIS IS MY brother Sam, who I was telling you about, who has over two million subscribers on YouTube," my eldest brother, Matthew, enthusiastically said as he introduced me to a friend. "He and his wife do YouTube for a *living*."

Among our close family and friends, Matthew stood out as our biggest support. I'd even venture to say he was our number-one fan. Fascinated by our meteoric rise on YouTube and always eager to join in on my wild video concepts, he proudly shared our accomplishments with anyone willing to listen.

Matthew monitored news articles about us and tracked our YouTube progress closer than we did ourselves. He even took the time and initiative to create a Wikipedia page in our honor, defending it from deletion on multiple occasions, believing Nia and I made a mark on the world that made us worthy of a permanent entry on the Internet.

Another brother would tease him, telling him he was obsessed with *Sam and Nia*. However, Matthew was more than just fascinated; he steadfastly stood by us, consistently offering his heartfelt love, encouragement, and advice like the best big brother you ever had. We could always find him in our corner.

On August 18th, 2015, two days before Nia and I were set to depart for VloggerFair, Matthew kept the family updated on two fronts: the views of our viral pregnancy video, which stood at 14 million views two weeks after its upload, and the news media's response to our pregnancy and miscarriage videos. But that wasn't all he shared with us. He also informed the family of an unrelated current event grabbing the world's attention.

A hacker group known as "The Impact Team" issued a public ultimatum exactly one month prior, demanding that the extramarital dating site Ashley Madison shut down by that very day. If the site failed to comply, the hackers threatened to leak 60 gigabytes of confidential user data to the world.

"Times up," Matthew texted. "Will Ashley Madison shut down their site, or will the hackers reveal the names of all the idiots who signed up to cheat on their spouse?"

By the end of the day, Matthew would tell us that the hackers followed through on their threat. The world was stunned by the sheer number of exposed adulterers. The account details of thirty-seven million users, which included names, addresses, sexual proclivities, and even private chats, were released to the public.

"The funniest part about all this," Matthew wrote, "is only one percent of the accounts belong to real women."

As prominent names emerged from the leak, dominating social media discussions and making headlines worldwide, it fueled more lively texts from Matthew. "The poor wives!" He wrote. "I hope all these men get found out and there's genuine repentance, but these guys deserve exactly what they have coming."

Several family members responded to Matthew's Ashley Madison commentary, agreeing with his sentiments and adding their own thoughts and disgust towards it. I, on the other hand, remained silent, dreading that my number one fan, Matthew, not to mention the rest of my family, seemed to be on the brink of a profound disappointment. The chances were growing that they'd soon discover a sister-in-law was among the "poor wives" that Matthew pitied.

As I followed Nia through the corridors of DFW Airport, I incessantly checked my phone for new information about the hack. A second massive data dump was scheduled to be released sometime that day. I was starting to sweat.

"I think I want to eat here," Nia said, stopping in front of a Chili's restaurant.

"Okay," I said, indifferent.

As Nia picked up a menu and began browsing through it, I leaned against a wall and tried desperately to remember the details of the day I had created my own Ashely Madison account two years prior. I recalled that I was sitting at my nurse's desk during a night shift when an ad for the site caught my attention, but I couldn't recall more important details, such as whether or not I used my real information.

Despite desperately wanting not to revisit it, my mind drifted back to the most reckless and regretful period of my life. Then, a pivotal detail surfaced. An old nursing colleague accused me of a heinous act I hadn't committed. While she was wrong about the specifics, her instincts weren't far off.

****

I was administering anti-nausea medication to a vomiting patient when the charge nurse, Michelene, pulled back the curtain and beckoned me out of the room.

"This better be important," I mumbled.

After following her to the nurse's desk, she pointed at a computer monitor sitting on the desk. Three other staff members sat nearby, clearly anticipating a response from me. I looked at the screen and saw it was filled with pop-up ads featuring explicit photos of women.

"Okay?" I scornfully replied. Little did anyone know I was already frustrated inside about an entirely different yet somewhat related matter.

Michelene cleared her throat. "Well, you were the last person sitting there," she said, "so you tell me."

I pulled off my latex gloves and threw them on the desk. "Do you really think I'm that stupid to pull up pornography on a work computer right here in the open, Michelene?" I loudly asked. A curious doctor peeked his head out from inside his office.

Michelene shrugged her shoulders. "I don't know, Sam," she said as she walked away.

With an eye roll, I powered off the computer, knowing it was just a virus, and then returned to my patient's room. While programming an IV pump, my thoughts drifted back to where they were before Michelene interrupted me.

Why would I waste my money on such a stupid app? I barked at myself.

As I jabbed the start button on the pump harder than necessary, I acknowledged that I deserved no better than to be accused of looking at pornography at work.

I've turned into the exact person who I never wanted people to think I was. "How did I get here?" I whispered. I had everything a man could ever dream of waiting for me at home, yet there I was, jeopardizing everything on a site made for adulterers.

Michelene pinpointed me for precisely the man I am.

Once the Phenergan took effect for my patient, I went to the far end of the nurse's station, distancing myself from the co-workers who rightfully suspected me of betraying my wife but accused me of a far less severe act than the ones I was actually guilty of.

As I sank into my chair, I felt as empty as the inbox in my Ashley Madison app. The hard-hitting awareness of blatantly searching for an affair, mixed with the reality of being rejected by every woman the sleazy site attracted, along with the sudden realization that I was giving off the vibe of a scumbag husband, sickened me. A severe intestinal blockage, like the one my patient had, suddenly seemed like a vacation compared to the condition of simply being myself.

My guilt intensified even more when I thought about Nia soon giving birth to our second child, my first son, and how my actions risked my children being raised in a broken home like I had been. That was my breaking point. I was done with the reckless lifestyle I had been leading.

Buried beneath a clutter of miscellaneous apps, I clicked on the solid black icon, launching the AM app on my iPhone. My head shaking with disgust, I navigated to account settings and authorized one final payment to have my account permanently erased from the AM database. I then uninstalled the app, closing that chapter of my life for good.

This isn't me, I told myself. *I'm done.*

****

I took a deep breath and let out a huge sigh of relief after recalling that I had hard-deleted my account.

My secrets are safe, I assured myself.

I shut down the private browsing windows on my iPhone, where I'd been searching for names linked to the AM breach, then hopped onto Twitter to check out the buzz about the upcoming VloggerFair events.

My attention was quickly diverted to a suspicious notification.

(Nia)

Once we got through airport security—my bag being pulled aside for a hand check as seemed to always be my luck—my stomach started to growl at me even louder. After all the dental work I'd undergone, I hadn't eaten a full meal all day, and now it was 6 pm, and I was starving. Walking to our gate, a Chili's restaurant got my attention.

Before settling at a table, I pored over the menu, intent on selecting the ideal dish to break my fast. Still absorbed in his phone, Sam stood leaning against the wall several feet away.

After deciding that Chili's was where I'd silence my hunger pains, I gestured to the host to tell her I was ready to be seated.

Seeking his attention, I said, "Sam, come on," playfully adding, "I need *food*!"

When he looked up from his phone, his face was pale.

13
Shattered

You will say, "How I hated discipline! If only I had not ignored all the warnings! ...now I must face public disgrace."
Proverbs 5:12-14

(Sam)

THE NOTIFICATION READ: "@Fu***ardidiot mentioned you in a tweet." My throat tightened as I tapped it open. I read the tweet that filled my screen: "Oh hey sam rader the viral miscarriage guy is on the Ashley Madison dump. Did I scoop this?"

I looked up from my phone, and my ears started ringing

The words hit me like an unexpected punch to the stomach and a kick to the back. My eyes bounced back and forth rapidly in their sockets, vibrating the bustling airport around me into a nightmarish blur. I bore down and exhaled through my tightening airway, trying to bring my iPhone screen back into focus.

"Oh my gosh! oh my gosh!" I muttered quietly, my voice strained and breathless. *Please, God, no,* I prayed. *Please, no.*

I read it again: "Sam Rader..." *No, no, no...* "Ashley Madison..." *This can't be happening...* My heart slammed into my rib cage.

I fumbled to tap open an image attached to the tweet. I zoomed in. It revealed a screenshot of a list of financial transactions. "Samuel Rader,

Samuel Rader, Samuel Rader," I read typed out beside each entry. *This can't be real.* The email I used to open the account was listed as well: *Samuel@BecauseThatsWhy.com.* As the public owner of the site Becausethatswhy.com, I realized that proving the account wasn't mine would be nearly impossible. *I'm done.*

My knees became weak, and I felt blood rush out of my face. I dropped my head and could see my heart palpating on the outside of my shirt. I felt the need to swallow but couldn't. *I used my real information?!* I found myself between bouts of gasping for air and holding my breath, trying desperately not to lose consciousness.

Your life is over. This is it. You're done.

A gut-wrenching sensation twisted inside me as though I were being forced to surrender control of my life to some unseen force. My mind flooded with thoughts of Nia. She seemed to be the only person I had left on my side since the pregnancy and miscarriage rumors started, and now I was on the verge of losing her. A deep, painful sense of loneliness engulfed me. God had given me multiple chances to come clean to her about my struggles, but I treated them all as mere suggestions. I was dead set on never telling Nia anything about my dark past, and now, it seemed, God was exposing it to everyone.

My panic sparked a haunting memory of a previous episode when I found myself in a strikingly similar situation, on the edge of my sexual struggles being exposed. It was the only other instance where, at least for a moment, I was convinced that both Nia's life and mine were over.

****

While Nia slept peacefully beside me, I lay awake in our bed, overcome by the familiar whirlwind of anxious thoughts: *I don't want to go to work tomorrow. I can't stand working for Michelene. How am I going to pay for our failing AC unit? I need to get the lawn mowed. I need to spend more time with the kids. I need to work out more.*

After an hour of staring through the ceiling, I carefully slipped out of bed for a trip to the guest restroom down the hall from our bedroom, grabbing my phone on the way despite the temptations I knew it would bring. I let the bathroom door silently latch behind me, hiding myself within the walls of my private sanctuary. Sitting down, I assured myself, *just a quick scroll through Facebook and nothing more.* Mere minutes into my solitude, after seeing an inappropriate photo of a woman on Facebook, my actions betrayed my intentions.

With a quick, experienced tap of my finger, I activated private browsing on Safari and keyed in a single word: "porn." One of the suggested adult sites caught my attention, offering the immediate escape I sought. I let myself be absorbed, disconnecting my mind from my worries and surroundings. Then, suddenly...

"CRASH!"

A chilling sound broke through the silence of our home. A blood-curdling combination of shattering glass and a high-pitched scream coming from the depths of Nia's lungs startled me so badly that after jolting me off the toilet, I nearly dove head-first into the bathtub.

"What the heck?!" I screamed. My eyes, trying to keep up with the sudden surge of adrenaline, rattled back and forth like earthquakes in my head. My mind immediately jumped to the worst-case scenario: someone had broken in through our bedroom window and was attacking Nia.

Driven by a whole other instinctive panic of potentially being caught, I stuffed my phone into the folded towels on the shelf before me. After struggling to pull up my shorts, I yanked open the bathroom door, revealing a dark hallway that now seemed impossibly long, twisting and shifting like a dizzying vortex tunnel. All I could see was a dark hole at the end of the hall, a gateway to my inevitable death.

Nia drew in a sharp breath, followed by another scream. I put one foot in front of the other as if balancing on a tightrope, stretching out my arms to the walls on either side to keep from tumbling to the ground. I was in the throes of an intense episode of psychological shock.

As I crossed the threshold of our bedroom, I was certain that I was about to witness the unthinkable: my wife being murdered. As my eyes adapted to the sudden light after flipping on the switch, I saw Nia sitting upright in the center of our bed, her eyes as wide as I had ever seen them. My gaze darted around the room as I hurried to her side and vaulted onto the bed. I drew Nia into a protective hold.

"What's happening?!" Nia screamed through a stream of tears.

"It's okay, it's okay," I said.

After ensuring no one else was in the room, I glanced at the floor and understood what happened. I took a deep breath and slowly released it, trying to lower my blood pressure. Nia's frantic sobbing persisted.

"Everything's okay, cutie," I said, still trying to catch my breath. "Our dresser mirror fell."

"What?" She asked, "How?"

I got off the bed as if to inspect the shattered mirror, then squatted beside it at the foot of the bed. I stared into my reflection in a shard of glass and knew that I was looking at a warning from God. I heard a voice inside me demand, *confess it to her now.* A whole other terror came over me.

Despite my fear of God, my fear of shattering Nia proved stronger. I told Nia I had been using the restroom when the incident happened, adding the lie that I hadn't even had time to wipe. Before returning to bed, I returned to the restroom and erased all evidence of my wrongdoing.

Usually, broken glass, let alone a giant shattered mirror spread across every square inch of the floor, would have gotten my immediate attention. But on that night, the scattered glass wasn't as important to me as what it represented. It reminded me of the life Nia and I still had. I left the pieces on the floor to be cleaned up the next day and turned off our light.

As I lay beside Nia, both of us still recovering from shock, I silently reflected. The old, heavy mirror had been resting on our dresser, leaning against the wall, securely for years, never once showing signs of instability. The realization that there was no explanation for it falling to the floor sent chills down my spine. Before closing my eyes, I vowed to God never to look at pornography again, missing the opportunity to potentially avoid truly shattering both Nia's life and my own five years down the road.

****

I tapped open replies. The first reply came from the author of the tweet. It read, "Please do not tag Sam and his wife on this! If she wants to know, she should Learn To Code." It seemed like a glimmer of hope. As I read the next reply, "Single best tweet in this entire leak," an overwhelming sense of doom coursed through me as if I had just run my car off an unfinished bridge. The next replier suggested someone might have fraudulently used my information to sign up—another glimmer of hope.

I glanced up at the bustling airport. "What the heck do I do?" I said aloud. The vibrant ads plastered across the walls transported me back to when I first heard about Ashley Madison. It was an advertisement that sold me on the lie that having an affair was simple and harmless, the thing people did before they died. "Life is short," they reminded, "Have an affair," they suggested. I was witnessing firsthand that the opposite was true. Infidelity didn't add spice to life; it invited chaos.

I had realized and embraced, long before this moment, that when God commanded, "Thou shalt not commit adultery," it wasn't merely a rule for His own benefit but primarily for mine. It was a loving caution against trying to defy the laws of nature. Essentially, He told me, "Don't jump off that cliff because you can't fly." Instead of heeding His instructions and trusting the maker of the universe, I jumped, flapped my arms as fast as I could, and still hit the ground at full force. When I broke His commandment, it broke me, not Him.

Nia stared at me from the entrance of the Chilli's restaurant. Her lips were moving, but I couldn't hear a word. As she ventured into the dark restaurant, I followed.

Sitting beside her in the small booth, I felt compelled to tell her about the revelations on my phone before hers did it for me. As if it had ever done any good for me in the past, I told myself that only a portion of the truth would be bearable in our already complex situation. Nia deserved none of the burden I was going to unload on her slender shoulders, let alone the complete truth. I resolved to lessen the blow, deciding to reveal the absolute minimum necessary and, once again, crafted a lie.

14
Daddy's Not Home

*The prudent sees danger and hides himself,
but the simple go on and suffer for it.*
Proverbs 22:3

(Nia)

"ARE YOU READY to order?" The waitress asked.

Sam flung open the menu, pointed at the first photo that caught his eye, and then returned to looking at his phone.

"I'll take the cajun chicken pasta with extra tomatoes, please," I said. As the waitress walked away, I turned to Sam. "What's going on?" I asked.

"Give me a minute, cutie," he said, maintaining focus on his phone. I noted that his tone was serious as I snacked on chips and salsa while waiting for his response.

Taking a deep breath, Sam looked up from his phone and into my eyes. He scooted closer and leaned in. Sensing his next words were going to be important, I set down the chip that I was bringing to my mouth. "What is it?" I asked.

"I have to tell you something," he said.

"Okay, tell me already," I laughed.

"Okay, so, two years ago, when I was a nurse," he began, "I made an account on an app called Ashley Madison."

"Okay?" I said, confused by the seemingly random words. "What's that?"

"It's like a dating app but for married people," he mumbled, looking down at the table.

"It's what?!" I asked, throwing my head back, nearly giving myself whiplash.

"It's a cheating app for married people," he said.

Not comprehending what I was hearing or why, I said, "Are you serious?!"

"But I never did anything on it," he added. "I made an account out of curiosity and boredom while I was at work one night and deleted it a few weeks later."

The waitress returned with our meals. "Can I get you guys anything else?" she asked after setting down our plates.

"We're fine," Sam said, "Thanks."

My stomach sank as I let his words sink in, and just like that, my appetite, my trip, and my marriage were ruined.

Sam continued with his confession, but I could no longer look at him. In a panic-like state, he explained that the company had been hacked and that the account he had created had just been made public and was currently being talked about on Twitter. What I heard louder than his words, however, were my thoughts.

I knew he was keeping something from me.

"What are you thinking?" Sam asked.

I was shocked, but a small part of me wasn't surprised. "Don't make me talk right now," I said angrily. I picked up my fork and bit into my pasta to keep from shouting at him.

Sam emphasized again that he had never had an affair and that the most he ever did on the site was send a couple of short messages. He told me matter-of-factly that I had nothing to be concerned about except for the fact that the account had just been made public.

As I continued to pick at my meal, trying to allow Sam's reassuring words to quell the storm inside me, I shook my head as I thought back to the first time I started sensing Sam was keeping something from me.

Why did I not listen to my intuition? I thought.

****

Two weeks into being a new mother, the fresh, sugary scents of baby lotion and powder in the air, I rested on our cool leather couch with my tiny newborn curled up in my arms. I was in love as I held my dream come true, Symphony Pearl Rader, and felt a strong sense of pride after having taken care of her alone, without Sam, all day for the first time since her birth.

"I hope you're ready for Daddy's big kisses, baby bear," I whispered before softly kissing Symphony's tiny ear.

It was Sam's first day back to nursing school since the birth of our first baby, and my heart fluttered as the time for him to come home grew closer. I just knew he was also counting down the seconds to be with us. I married my high school sweetheart, and we created a home together, and now we had our first baby. Life was perfect.

Being careful not to further strain my two torn C-section stitches, I changed Symphony's diaper and then placed her in her pink rocker. I eased myself onto the couch beside her and watched with a big smile as colorful lights rolled over her tiny face while the rocker soothed her to sleep.

As I heard Sam climb the porch stairs and make his way through the squeaky storm door, I tussled my hair and thought, *will he sit by me and ask about all the cute baby details of the day?* He now had *two* ladies looking forward to his return. *How will this go?!* I was so excited to start a new, sweet family routine.

Seconds later, the hero of our day walked through the door in his all-white scrubs and five-o'clock shadow; the perfect picture of "Daddy's home!"

"Hey, cutie,' he said as he entered.

"Hi!" I said excitedly. "You're home..." My voice trailed off as I watched him walk past me and then the baby, heading through the kitchen straight to his office. I expected he would return after dropping off his bag, but instead, I heard him settle into his chair and roll it under his desk. It marked a heartbreaking turning point for me.

I sat there in disbelief, feeling hot tears sting the back of my eyes as I stared at Symphony, wondering how her daddy could just walk past her without so much as a kiss. My heart ached for us.

When I shared my feelings with him that night in bed, he explained that the stress of his new assignments had overwhelmed him. He apologized and assured me that our sacrifices would pay off in the long run. He asked for my patience as he dealt with the pressures of nursing school for the next two years.

As I tried to fall asleep while trying to accept my new reality, I silently wept. Sam went to school with mostly women, and I couldn't help but feel he was giving them his better side. Sam may have been back to the house, but *Daddy* wasn't exactly *home*.

I decided to trust that Sam was being careful not to give away what was rightfully mine and our daughters and did my best to put on the front of an understanding wife. I eventually adapted to our new way of life. I didn't realize, however, that this was merely the first domino of many to fall, each one faster than the last.

As time passed, I continuously had to lower my expectations at Sam's request, causing me many nights of disappointment and tears as I watched our marriage fail at being like the one I witnessed with my Me-me and Pappy. I found myself falling asleep on a regular occurrence to the same prayer: *God, please get me out of this sad place.*

****

"Please tell me what you're thinking, cutie," Sam begged.

Still shaking my head, not breaking eye contact with my pasta, I finally replied, "I always knew something was off. I guess I'm glad to know I wasn't crazy."

"I'm really sorry," Sam said, almost hyperventilating. "It was so, so stupid."

After offering several more apologies and reassuring words, Sam dropped his head on the table and insisted that our biggest worry should be the potential public exposure. He was adamant that once the news started spreading, our channel would not survive, and his chances of finding work again would be impossible due to his damaged reputation.

"Should we still go to VloggerFair?" Sam asked. "I'm sure everyone will know before we even land."

"Do you think I want to take what you just told me, go home, and take care of a house and two kids?" I snapped. "Of course, I'm going!"

"Okay," he mumbled.

Observing Sam in a state of panic oddly helped me maintain my composure. He was already experiencing the consequences of his actions without me having to do anything. For a moment, I felt like the hackers were fighting in my corner. His panic seemed so over the top that even though I had more of a right to be upset than he did, I started feeling sorry for him and even found it in myself to try to help him.

"Are you sure you never met with anyone?" I asked.

"No, I swear," Sam responded. "I had the account for maybe a month, then deleted it. I never once saw anyone."

"If you didn't meet with anyone and signed up for it years ago," I explained, "then I don't think it'll be as big a deal as you think."

"Yeah, maybe," he said, taking a deep breath.

"So, just calm down," I said.

Maybe it was out of habit, or perhaps my trust in this man ran that deep, but I believed every word Sam told me. He said it was just a moment of dumb curiosity that amounted to nothing, and I accepted that. Besides, despite what I was learning, there was one thing I knew for sure: Sam truly loved me.

"Thank you, cutie," Sam responded, "I'm so sorry I did this."

I asked, "How will people even know it's actually your account anyway?"

"Yeah," Sam began, "I'm reporting anyone who tweets about it, but I used my real information when I signed up, so it's hard to prove they're lying." He told me he needed to call his brothers for their help, covering up the fact that he owned the site to which his email was attached. He frantically typed on his phone, stood up, and left the restaurant.

Sitting alone in the booth, I thought more about Sam's Ashley Madison account. My anger quickly started to grow. Not only had he allowed his mind to consider cheating on me, but I was potentially on the verge of public embarrassment because of it.

Questions began firing off in my brain, one after the next, each feeling like a stinging slap to my face. *Why wasn't I enough?*

He had signed up for the account a month before the birth of our second child. *Why wasn't he thinking about his son? I know we were having less sex, but I never left him unsatisfied.*

As Sam and I boarded the plane, I was torn between not wanting to speak to him and having a thousand questions to ask. But the moment we sat down, side by side, Sam made it evident that he was still panicking inside. He persisted in knowing if I forgave him and if I'd still have his back if his AM account made the news when we landed.

"Yes," I told him, "I'll be able to get past it, but right now, I just want to be alone." He then moved to a vacant seat several rows in front of me.

A film I had been wanting to see was playing on the screen in front of me: *Far from the Madding Crowd*. I plugged in my headphones, looking forward to a break from Sam's panic and my new reality. I was met with a dreary love triangle full of romantic chaos and betrayal, pushing me further into sadness. The good guy eventually got the girl, but not before there were broken hearts.

Was Sam the good guy or the bad guy? I wondered.

15

Untying the Knot

*God destroys those who speak lies
and abhors the deceitful man.*
Psalms 5:6

(Sam)

LEAVING NIA SITTING alone amplified my feelings of failure. I wanted to be next to her to fight off intruders in her mind, like the lie that she wasn't enough, but I found my own mind was under attack. *Who am I to think I can protect Nia from lies when I'm the biggest liar of all?*

I pressed my forehead against the seat in front of me, dug my arms into my knotted-up stomach, and grimaced into a prayer: *Please, God, be with Nia. Let her be comforted by your unfailing love. Forgive me for not keeping her safe and feeling cherished.*

I couldn't shake the thought that, because of my selfish actions, Nia was left feeling just as ashamed as I was, if not more so. I started berating myself and hating who I was as a person, a feeling reminiscent of my past that always emerged after succumbing to temptations and, in turn, would make me all the more vulnerable to repeating them. The last thing I wanted was to get caught up in that downward spiral after so many years of God setting me free from it, especially when Nia needed me most.

I pleaded with God to help Nia and me to see ourselves as He sees us—chosen, set apart, overcomers, and loved. *Let me draw my strength from you, Lord,* I prayed. *I can't carry this heavy cross without you.* But the intrusive thoughts returned the moment I said amen.

A disturbing experience from five years prior made its way to the surface of my mind in vivid detail, tormenting me even further and reminding me of the selfishness and recklessness I was capable of.

Everyone would be better off right now if I hadn't survived that night, I thought.

****

I repeated my evening plans, "I'm meeting Mitch at his house to study for our nursing exam, and then we're going straight to the movies from there."

"Well, okay," Nia said, looking at the floor. "We're just really going to miss you."

With a gentle pull, I embraced her and our one-year-old daughter and kissed them both on the cheek. Over Nia's shoulder, I whispered, "I love you," as I gazed at our wedding photo, taken a year earlier, hanging on the wall directly in front of me.

An unsettling feeling crept over me. *Don't leave.*

"I'll call you in the morning before class," I said as I released her. "It's only one night."

As we stood there, gazing into each other's eyes, I sensed she could tell something was off. My heart rate increased as the truth hung in the balance. Nia would only ignore tension between us when we were parting ways, assuming any goodbye could be our last. Using this to my advantage, I quickly opened the front door.

"Bye, cutie," I said. "I love you."

With a big, bright smile, she said, "I love you, too." Then she kissed me on the lips.

I slid into my green Toyota Corolla, gripping the cracked steering wheel. Just as I was closing the car door, Nia flung open the glass storm door of the house and shouted, "We'll miss you, manly!" I gave the horn a couple of light taps, then closed my door.

You don't have to do this, I told myself as I started the car.

Already weighed down by guilt from previous deceptions, I felt too defeated to resist my natural inclinations toward more selfish pleasure-seeking.

It's too late now.

Sam and Nia | Live in Truth

I shifted the gear into drive and drifted away from my home and whatever wisdom I had left.

Six hours later, I found myself cramped behind the passenger seat of Mitch's gray Toyota Tundra. Jimmy, our designated driver, had indulged in more alcohol than he let on. It was 3 AM, and we were heading home after a night of excess. I had just wasted Nia's and my money on alcohol and lap dances and was determined to protect her from ever knowing. To cover it up, I deviously looked up several synopses and plot spoilers for the movie I had lied to Nia about seeing that night, committing them to memory in case she asked about it when I returned home the following day.

Jimmy, leaning over the steering wheel, stared deep into the empty highway ahead as it hypnotizingly passed under us at 75 miles per hour. *Looks like he's getting sleepy,* I thought. Our exit ramp was approaching—the same kind of bridge that terrified Nia —that soared four lanes into the air, aptly named the Texas-style Stack. "Slow down, Sam!" Nia never failed to demand from me when driving over one.

Pushing my forehead against the small, damp window beside me as we took our exit, I thought about the life I had built. It wasn't the life of fame I once dreamed of; I never got that record deal, saw my name in lights, heard the thunderous ovations, or achieved any form of widely celebrated success. *I'm still in Texas,* I thought, *worlds away from where dreams come true.* I never did make it to "Cali for Nia," the title of a song I wrote for Nia in high school. My thoughts then drifted to her.

Nia was my rock, my favorite thing about a life that otherwise didn't go as planned. She was the only thing that really worked out for me. Yet there I was, risking the single most beautiful thing I had in my life.

You're such a fool, I told myself. Then everything changed.

"Screech!!" The sound of skidding tires pierced the night, snapping me out of my regretful thoughts. I was pulled to the opposite end of the truck cab by some invisible force. My eyes darted to Jimmy, whose knuckles and face were white as he clung to the steering wheel as the truck lurched back and forth along the center of the bridge. The guardrails on either side seemed to act as magnets to the truck. The smell of burning rubber grew stronger.

Again, my body was thrust against the truck's wall, prompting me to steal a quick glance out of my side window. *This is it,* I thought, glaring over the guardrail at the ground several stories below.

After another swerve, Jimmy lost the battle.

With the jarring sound of metal meeting concrete, we slammed into the barrier on the front passenger side of the truck. My body was thrust toward the impact into the back of the passenger seat. The truck rebounded off the guardrail back into the center of the bridge. Jimmy hit the brakes, and the truck came to a stuttering stop, eerily resting at the peak of the ramp in a cloud of smoke. Everything was suddenly quiet, my mind suspended between death and salvation.

Did we really just survive that? I asked myself.

Jimmy broke the silence. "Is everyone okay?"

Mitch nodded.

"I'm fine," I said.

We all climbed out of the truck. Stepping over shards of glass as Mitch and Jimmy inspected the damage, I walked to the edge where the collision occurred. In a whisper, looking down at the ground several stories below, I said, "Thank you, God," followed by a heartfelt, "I'm so stupid."

Mitch pulled the passenger seat down to allow me to reenter. "Don't worry," Jimmy told Mitch as he climbed in, "I'll get it fixed."

Once I settled into my seat, I felt a small, loose object rattling inside my shoe.

"Oh no," I said aloud. Shock and panic returned with a vengeance. The relief of surviving the accident vanished in an instant.

I threw my foot onto the seat beside me and untied the knot.

Oh my gosh, I thought, squeezing my eyes shut as I reached into my shoe.

As I pulled out my hand and looked at the small item resting in my palm, I found myself emotionally powerless, breaking down in tears as if I were the only person in the truck. Mitch turned around and looked at me "We're okay, buddy," he said. He had no idea.

Not only had I been mere inches away from meeting my creator after a night of debauchery, but I had also left Nia behind with an endless number of questions, the foremost being, "Why was his wedding ring in his shoe?"

****

As we hit turbulence, I glanced over to check on Nia. I was thankful to see that she was watching a movie, hoping it was providing her an escape. However, there was no denying the sadness in her eyes.

The most joyful woman I had ever known, with the noblest character of anyone I've ever met and overflowing with a contagious kindness, now looked utterly dejected. She barely knew a fraction of the truth, yet I felt I had already marred one of God's most prized possessions.

I was grateful to have been able to tell Nia truthfully that I hadn't met up with anyone through the site, but this was not due to any noble decision on my part. Had the chance to meet someone arisen, I would have taken it. Signing up for Ashley Madison was just a small part of the destructive cycle I was caught up in at the start of our marriage. Its only true significance lay in that it was my final attempt—after numerous failed ones—to find something beyond disappointment and shame in the arms of a woman who wasn't my wife.

16
Tempo Change

*Look at those who are honest and good,
for a wonderful future awaits those who love peace.
Psalm 37:37*

(Nia)

THE PLANE LANDED, and despite having to give up the safety of my own row of seats, landing in Seattle brought me a sigh of relief. I had managed to survive the turbulence of transitioning from a happy marriage to a questionable one.

Sam moved back to sitting next to me as the plane taxied. He asked me how I was feeling. "Okay, I guess," I said. After my movie had ended, prayer softened my heart. It felt bruised but not broken. I had prepared myself to be receptive to Sam's apologies and show him grace.

"Well, I just hope you know how much I love you," he said. "Please believe me when I say that I want no one but you, and I've never wanted to leave you for another woman. It was just a stupid curiosity that led to nothing."

I believed him. "Okay," I said, closing my eyes and resting my head on the back of my seat.

"Do you forgive me?" he asked.

I pursed my lips, giving the question thought even though I already knew the answer.

"I truly am sorry," he added. "That is not the man I am at all anymore."

"I do," I said, "but I'm still sad about it."

Sam wrapped his arms around me and put his forehead against mine. He thanked me and promised me that our love had always been real.

"What's happening on Twitter?" I asked.

"Well," He began as he sat up, "The tweets have slowed down."

"That's good," I said

"Josh Duggar issued a statement almost instantly after his name was found," Sam said, "and that's when the media took off with it. I'm thinking if I don't give it any attention, it won't go anywhere."

"That makes sense," I said.

In Seattle, we were set to stay at an Airbnb with some friends. For the first night, however, Sam and I stayed at a hotel. Lying on the king-sized bed of our room, trying to recalibrate after the deep talk Sam and I had in our rental car on the way over, I texted Chantel. After bringing her up to speed, Pastor Bo called Sam. Sam put him on speakerphone. I listened as Bo asked Sam if he truly hadn't met with anyone. After Sam reassured him of his minimal interaction on the site, Bo asked me where I stood in terms of forgiving him.

"I forgive him," I said. "I'm disappointed, but the news didn't break me or anything."

"Then you guys need to move forward and be committed to walking through whatever might happen next, hand in hand," Bo said. "If this picks up steam, there will be a lot coming your way. Let's pray."

I felt a sense of accomplishment after we hung up. I had finally discovered what had been gnawing at my intuition for years and handled it with Godliness and maturity. I was proud to uphold the "through thick" part of our wedding vows, even after Sam hadn't. Since our wedding day, I had always been aware that such marital conflicts would eventually emerge. As I got ready for bed, memories of that day returned to me, and I recalled how I had mentally prepared myself for the very challenge I found myself living in.

****

On September 12th, 2009, five years after our first kiss, Sam and I would be sharing another first kiss. It was the day I had fantasized about since I was a little girl: my wedding day.

Despite waking up to an overcast sky with rain in the forecast, I refused to worry. Every detail, down to the last flower petal, had been meticulously chosen, and I was determined not to let anything come between it.

"Should we move it to the church?" my friend Katie asked as she looked up at the gray clouds overhead.

"Nope," I insisted. "It won't rain." God knew how important the day was for me. He wouldn't allow it.

As 6 PM approached, with my cousin styling my hair and my handwritten vows in hand, an overwhelming realization washed over me. I was seconds away from finally becoming a wife. I couldn't hold back the tears. My dreams were coming true.

Sam's eldest brother, Matthew, was our photographer. A friend from school served as our usher and DJ, and a friend's grandmother made our five-layer cake, symbolizing our five-year relationship. Sam and his dad built our dance floor. Our childhood pastor and English teacher, Mr. Mabe, would officiate. Our loved ones surrounded us, making every part of the day personal and memorable.

"You may kiss the bride," Brother Tim announced. Sam held my face and kissed me like he never wanted it to end. It was the first kiss of the rest of our lives.

We stood under the house's entrance awning, basking in warm hugs and congratulations from friends and family. When I wasn't caught up in the embraces, my eyes were irresistibly drawn to Sam, my husband.

"I love you," I mouthed as Sam hugged an old high school friend.

Almost everyone was amazed that we had dodged the forecasted rain, adding an extra layer of magic to our special day. "Remember, guys," a friend playfully warned us, "God won't always prevent the rain from pouring on your marriage." The rest of our wedding day would prove that wisdom to be correct.

Due to the extra moisture in the air, our wedding cake started leaning. We forgot to hand out the wedding programs that we had worked tirelessly on. Sam's best man, his twin brother, gave a speech that was about as unprepared as the line for the finger foods. During our first dance, the rain poured down on us, soaking my new wedding dress and drenching the dance floor. Despite it all, my wedding still felt utterly perfect.

Neither my wet hair nor my squishy shoes mattered. In that fairytale moment, dancing in the rain to *When God Made You* by Newsong and Natalie Grant, it felt like Sam and I were the only two souls in existence. Sam's and my gaze were locked into each other, reaching my heart and filling me with an even greater desire for him.

As the song ended, Sam turned away, smiling at our family and friends, who had begun to applaud. A wave of clarity swept over me: our marriage wouldn't be perfect, but its uniqueness would make it all the more precious, just like our wedding day.

I was fully committed, ready to fight for this love, no matter what lay ahead. Marriage was what I had witnessed and looked up to in my Me-me and Pappy growing up. Their perseverance through hard times was why their marriage had always looked so beautiful to me.

I was so caught up in the moment that I barely noticed when the music changed tempo and others started to join us on the dance floor. Looking around at our friends and family celebrating with us in the rain, I realized this grand moment was not just a celebration but also a symbol of the storms we would inevitably face together in the years to come but would never have to do alone. At that moment, I was almost as excited for the rain that awaited us as I was for the clear skies.

****

My attitude towards Sam was genuine. I believed the dust would settle quickly, and I wanted to be there to reassure him of that. If things were to go south, I was ready to publicly defend Sam's character, our relationship, and our faith if necessary. Regardless of what was going to happen, I wanted him to bounce back as soon as possible so we could get back to living our fun YouTube life together. So, despite Sam's panic and considering all the what-ifs, I became more encouraging to Sam by the hour.

Determined not to let the oncoming public judgment break us and to show Sam that I would remain united with him throughout it all, we reconnected by sharing an intimate moment together.

17
Mocking Forgiven

Therefore, whatever you have said in the dark shall be heard in the light, and what you have whispered in private rooms shall be proclaimed on the housetops.
Luke 12:3

(Sam)

AFTER A CATHARTIC EVENING with Nia, which filled me with renewed hope for our marriage and YouTube channel, we were convinced we had nothing to worry about—that is until the sun came up.

The following morning, media requests for my response to the Ashley Madison allegations came pouring in by the dozen, abruptly plunging me back into a whirlpool of worry. One email, in particular, alarmed me more than the others.

It was from Aditi Roy from ABC News, the reporter who had covered our viral pregnancy video and the accusations that followed. She asked if we'd be willing to sit in front of their cameras once more to address my account, adding that they'd be postponing the broadcast of our segment, which had been scheduled to air that day, whether or not I chose to participate. They claimed the AM account allegations had become an integral part of our story and would be included in their piece about us.

Just two days prior, I had responded to Aditi Roy's question about the goal of our vlogs, stating it was to "shine God's light and deliver Christ's message to the world." That very same reporter was now questioning my faithfulness to my wife. I felt like a total fraud.

I never responded to ABC's or anyone else's request, believing they wouldn't legally be allowed to publish articles about my alleged involvement in the site without confirmation they were true. I was sadly mistaken.

At 2:30 PM on the first day of VloggerFair, Nia and I were seated in a conference room among other YouTube video creators, listening to YouTube guru Tim Shmoyer speak, when a friend in the row ahead turned around and held up his phone, signaling he had just sent me a text message.

"Oh great," I whispered to Nia, pulling my phone from my pocket.

I tapped on his message, and a link to a DailyMail article stared back at me. My heart, still surprisingly unaccustomed to the relentless surges of adrenaline, pounded inside me as Nia and I lipped the excessively long title: "*EXCLUSIVE: Father who "surprised" his wife with news she was pregnant then announced she had suffered a miscarriage was a paying user of Ashley Madison.*"

Nia looked up at me in disbelief. "Oh no," she said. "It'll be okay."

My iPhone vibrated again as more links to articles from the same YouTube friend flooded in, one after another, "Sam Rader" and "Ashley Madison" appearing in all the titles. After several minutes of trying to focus on Tim Schmoyer, feeling increasingly distracted by judgmental glares from every direction in the conference room, Nia and I decided the embarrassment was too unbearable and left the building.

"This is it, cutie," I said, "Our YouTube ride is over." The life of my dreams was crumbling before my eyes.

"Maybe not," Nia said, "let's just take it one step at a time."

"I'm so sorry I did this to us," I said, feeling undeserving of her encouragement.

Benji, from the YouTube channel ItsJudysLife, took me aside and offered me encouragement and advice, making me feel for the first time that day that not everyone was looking down on me. Then, after completing his presentation, Tim Schmoyer and his wife said a prayer over us.

As we drove back to the Airbnb, our confused emotions at an all-time high, I gave in to the mounting pressures from myself, our family, friends, and viewers and decided to shoot a response video for our channel addressing my account.

In the dimly lit living room of the small brick house we were renting, Nia and I settled onto the old, shag carpet in front of the couch, preparing to address what felt like the entire world. After propping our camera on a stack of throw pillows, I overlapped my shoulder with Nia's to fit us within the camera's view.

"It's too formal," I said. "I'll just hold it like it's any other vlog." My biggest goal was to conceal my panic as much as possible.

"Take a deep breath, cutie," Nia reminded me, gently rubbing my lower back.

Before pressing the camera's record button, I took one last look at the bullet points I jotted down on the ride over:

- *Introduce it*
- *Apologize for doing it*
- *Admit it was wrong, a complete mistake*
- *Clarify*
  - *It was long ago*
  - *I never met anyone*
  - *It was just a sinful curiosity*
  - *It's been resolved*
  - *I've gone to my pastor about it*
- *This is why we need Jesus.*
- *I've been forgiven and won't be discussing it further.*
- *This is what atonement is all about. We get second chances.*
- *Nia states marriage is worth fighting for.*

I raised the camera and hit record.

"Hey guys," I began. "As you may have seen, my name was associated with an Ashley Madison account. A website made for spouses who want to have an affair."

I was terrified of the possible additional backlash that would ensue if it came to light that Nia was unaware of the account before the hack, so I told our viewers she had already known about it and had worked through it. I claimed I had never had an affair, and then I told the most appalling lie of all—that I had already discussed the issue with my pastor, adding, "God has forgiven me."

To conclude the recording, I stressed that we would not speak of my AM account again.

I uploaded the video to the same channel that Nia and I treasured as our platform for sharing the life of a family devoted to living for God.

Then, as possibly the biggest mockery of all, I titled it *Forgiven*.

Receiving Nia's support and encouragement as I spewed out lies to our audience, making her complicit in my deceit, added to the mountain of shame I already bore. Had Nia been aware of the full extent of my betrayals, I would have been facing that camera alone.

Despite the surge of online articles, we remained actively involved in the conference after publishing the video, at one point, even participating in an onstage interview.

All day, I tried to suppress the growing tension within me, but when I encountered the two individuals who had publicly disagreed with my miscarriage tweet several days earlier, all the disappointment I had bottled up seemed to surface at once. They became the target of all my pent-up anger.

I was soon ejected from the conference for "threatening violence" after confronting the two individuals and demanding an explanation from them. While I never physically assaulted anyone, People.com released an article two days later titled, *Sam Rader Admits He Got Physical with Another Vlogger Before Being Thrown out of Convention.* I had given the media more fodder to further damage my reputation as a man of God.

The following night, I messaged the two individuals an apology. "I wish I could tell you in person, but I'm deeply sorry for the anger I showed towards you," I wrote. I explained that I'd be deactivating my Twitter account and then confessed that they and the rest of the public only knew a fraction of what Nia and I were actually going through.

PART 4
Parted Waters
The full confession

18
Live in Truth

The iniquities of the wicked ensnare him, and he is held fast in the cords of his sin.
Proverbs 5:22

(Sam)

I EXITED THE HIGHWAY, hoping a phone call with a friend would help slow down my escalating anxiety and accompanying nausea.

"Where are we going?" Nia asked softly.

"I need to pull over," I said. "I feel car sick."

Nia and I had just briefly discussed a text message sent to our family text group by my twin brother, who knew more about the double life I once lived than anyone else.

"Why are you still lying, bro?" he wrote. He was responding to the false claims I made in the *Forgiven* video.

"What's he talking about?" Nia asked.

Still trying to cover my tracks, I lied to Nia again, claiming I had no idea what my brother was referring to. The conviction of still lying to my wife with the same soul that loved Jesus created a painful conflict within me. I never intended to be weaving my web of lies after so many years since my last extramarital offense. I felt nauseous and claustrophobic.

I jerked the car to a stop at a curb in front of an abandoned storefront in a quiet part of downtown Seattle. Desperate to escape the suffocating bubble of thick guilt surrounding me, I flung open the driver's door, told Nia I would be calling Matthew, walked around the corner of the storefront, let out a huge sigh, and buckled at the waist as I grabbed my knees.

I can't do this, God. I prayed.

I remembered calling up my brother Matthew before boarding the plane to Seattle, informing him that my name had been exposed in the Ashley Madison leak. He seemed more astonished by the news than Nia. At first, he refused to believe it. "Oh, that's rich," Matthew replied with a laugh. "Can you imagine?" It was only after I sent him a screenshot of the tweet that first broke the news, proving what I was telling him wasn't a joke, that I heard his jaw drop on the other end. "I can't believe it. This can't be real, bro," he said, his voice reflecting my panic.

I decided to call him back and update him on my escalating situation.

"Dude," I said. "There's more that Nia doesn't know."

"Oh no, man. I figured there probably was," he responded, finishing a bite of something crunchy.

"I mean a lot more," I said, kicking at the sidewalk, feeling foolish for ever believing that I possessed some special immunity to the consequences of sin. "I'm sick of lying, bro," I said, "but there's just no way I can tell her everything." I paused. "It'll totally ruin her."

"I'm sorry you're going through this," Matthew said. "My heart is really hurting for Nia right now." He paused and added, "There's just no way around it. You have to tell her." He agreed that confessing it to Nia would probably break her but encouraged me to put the unknowns in God's hands.

"I don't think it's possible, bro," I replied.

After saying a prayer for me, we hung up.

For years, the burden of my secrets was something I thought I could bear. I had reconciled myself to the fact that they'd forever be a part of me. But like a slowly growing tumor on the back of my neck, it was beginning to cause me issues. I needed to make a choice: let it kill me or have it excised. I wanted to lean on Nia for support, as I always did. "What should I do, cutie?" I wanted to ask. But she was at the heart of my dilemma this time.

A couple strolled past me hand in hand, bringing to mind the searing memory of when, after a breakup in college, I spotted Nia walking out of a building with another man. Two days before, I had broken up with her because I wanted to "test the waters," thinking I could handle life without her. The sight of another man escorting Nia to her car killed me inside, proving I was lost without her. Seven years later, I found myself amid another emotional crisis, again possibly on the verge of completely losing Nia. I had promised to protect her heart if she gave me another chance. How could I have betrayed the trust she had reinstated in me back then?

I decided to call Pastor Bo.

As the ringback tones echoed in my ear, I silently counted them, hoping it would go to voicemail.

"Hey Sam, what's up?" Bo answered.

Great, I thought. *Now I have to say something.*

"Things are getting crazy over here," I said.

"One sec, let me go outside," he said. "How do you mean?" He asked.

I confessed to him that I'd been keeping many more secrets, ones far worse than the Ashley Madison account. I explained that they all took place many years ago before we started attending his church. "I'm a completely different person than I was back then," I told him. I argued that revealing them to Nia now would only resurrect a past that had long been buried.

"Can I just confess some things to you and let that be enough?" I begged.

Bo heard my desperate cries for what they were: a longing to be set free from the trap that I had ensnared myself in but fearful of the unknown world outside of it.

At first, the trap I was inadvertently setting for myself was concealed beneath the daily routines of life, each rope strand and weave representing a white lie or a poor decision. These small deceptions begot bigger ones, gradually increasing in size and number, making them heavier, more difficult to hide, and closer to activating the snare with its own weight. Yet, I carefully lived on top of it, adding more and more to its burden, purposefully looking away from the impending consequence. Then, one day, too heavy with the accumulated weight of my sins, the trap was triggered, leaving me dangling high up in the air in deep shame and regret, feeling hopeless that there was anything I could do to escape it.

Bo didn't waste time offering the solution to my panic. He went beyond mere prayers or vague counsel, issuing a three-word directive that resonated with such force and conviction that it felt like it had come directly from the Lord. "Sam," he began, his tone shifting from empathetic to imperative. I tensed, preparing myself for his wisdom.

"Yeah?" I said defeatedly.

"Live in truth."

His words, like they leaked out of heaven, struck me with the force of an unexpected embrace from behind. They startled me and nearly knocked my composure off of its feet.

Live in truth? It seemed too simple to seem so life-giving.

I had been walking through the wilderness, my enemy at my back, suddenly faced with a vast sea before me, resigned to the fate of being defeated and remaining in slavery. Then, Bo, following the Lord's command, lifted up his staff and split the waters, revealing there was a way out. It was the obvious path forward.

"Live in truth, brother," he repeated, this time with desperation in his voice.

This time, Bo's loving charge assured me that I wouldn't be alone in the world outside of my snare. He, Heath, Matthew, Dan, and many other men would be there to walk with me in the life of truth I was so afraid of. The moment felt so big I wondered if our whole YouTube journey had been nothing more than to lead me right where I stood, Bo in my ear, giving me these heavenly instructions.

Why hasn't a man told me this before? I wondered. *Live in Truth? What a concept.* Bo may as well have said, "Lazarus, come out." I felt like a new life was mere steps away.

I lifted my eyes to the sky, a huge lump in my throat, widening them to prevent tears from pouring out. With a voice shaking with emotion, I finally responded. "I can't even imagine what that's like, Bo," I said, "but it sounds amazing."

I had grown so accustomed to living in my snare that I had forgotten there was potentially a world for me outside of it. God granted me a small foretaste of that world through Bo's words. It tasted like pure, cold water to a dehydrated soul, drowning all guilt and fear hidden in all its crevices. I was left momentarily revitalized. All I had to do was submit, trust, and tell Nia everything to receive a full, lasting portion.

For the first time in my life, complete honesty with Nia seemed not only possible but necessary.

After Bo said a prayer and I gave him my heartfelt thanks, he said, "I'll see you guys when you get back home," reminding me again I wouldn't be going into the approaching fray without support.

I started walking back towards the car, glancing at Nia, who stood leaning against it, looking off into the distance, peacefully deep in thought. *Will this be the last time I see her like this,* I wondered, *blissfully unaware of my ugly secrets?* She radiated beauty and innocence, feeling wanted, accepted, and desired. Observing her frail frame as I drew closer, I realized I was witnessing the huge, albeit temporary, cost of living in truth.

19
Peace Illusion

Blessed are the peacemakers, for they shall be called sons of God.
Matthew 5:9

(Nia)

AS I SENSED SAM'S phone conversations winding down, I looked up from my phone, seizing a quiet moment to gather my thoughts before he returned to the car. I was eager to move past my frustrations with him for getting us kicked out of VloggerFair, so I had been preparing my heart to greet him with cheerfulness, hoping it would help us both reset and enjoy the rest of our evening together.

Like always, I wanted nothing more than for things to be smooth between us. I had this constant hope that in our marriage, we would make it a habit to be strong for each other whenever one of us was going through a hard time. Since Sam was experiencing a level of anxiety that was the most intense I'd ever seen, I decided it was time to practice those hopes and set aside my hurt and disappointments for the time being.

As I stood there gazing off into the distance, waiting for Sam to return, my mind raced back to a specific moment when I tried to be the change I wanted to see in my marriage. It made me question whether my peace-making strategies sometimes did more harm than good.

Peace Illusion

****

Sam returned home from nursing school looking exhausted. I hadn't seen him since he went to his friend Mitch's place the night before, and I'd been anxiously waiting for him to come home all day.

Walking in like a zombie, he tossed his books onto the couch, complaining of a headache. As much as I wanted to talk to him to settle my nerves, I gave him a kiss and watched him head to our bedroom.

As he slept, I carried on with my usual routine: caring for our one-year-old daughter, Symphony, tidying the house, folding laundry, etc. I was getting to play house in real life. But, this time, I was staying busy for different reasons. I sensed a change in Sam, first when he left the house the previous day and then when he returned.

When he began to stir from his nap, I felt a strong urge not to shy away from telling him what was on my heart. With a tightness in my chest, still unsure if I'd gain the courage to say anything, I put on a cartoon for Symphony and headed to our bedroom.

I snuggled up to Sam in bed as he recapped his day at school, looking for the right moment to mention the tension I sensed between us. I brought my face level with his, looking for clues in his expressions. Even when I got inches from his nose, he avoided eye contact, increasing my suspicions. After I gave him a big kiss on the mouth, I knew my intuition was correct: he had betrayed me.

In a brief moment of bravery, with the most innocent expression I could put on to soften the blow my words might have, I said, "I feel like you kissed someone last night."

With his grogginess unchanged, he said, "Well, I didn't, cutie." There was no trace of surprise or hint that he found the question unexpected or absurd. I didn't believe him. He was hiding something. Since he'd been on edge lately, stressed out with school and finances, I chose to shake off my suspicions.

"Well, okay," I said.

I left the room, pushing aside my doubts to keep the peace in our home. As uncomfortable as it was to dismiss my gut feelings, I trusted God, continued to pray for Sam, and then gathered ingredients for dinner.

****

I watched Sam approach the car, seemingly less tense than when we pulled over.

I guess the phone call helped, I thought.

I was excited to leave this all behind and enjoy a fun, memorable night with him before returning to our responsibilities at home the next day. "Are you ready to go?" I asked.

"I suppose," Sam said, returning a smile.

As if everything were back to normal, we re-entered the rental car and got back on the winding highway, headed for a devastating destination.

20
Trust Fall

*Fear not. These are the things that you shall do:
Speak the truth to one another.
2 Corinthians 3:16-18*

(Sam)

MY STOMACH CHURNED, but it wasn't car sickness; I had been holding down toxic secrets for years, and now my soul struggled to keep them from coming up.

"How did the phone call go?" Nia asked from the passenger seat.

"Good," I said, downplaying the life-changing nature of the call.

"Who did you talk to?" she asked. "What did they say?"

"Give me one sec, cutie," I replied.

I took in a deep breath and prayed against the sudden fear of cutting through ropes that bound me but also kept me safe from the unfamiliar territory outside it. I expected my secrets to be revealed *after* I died, in the privacy of God's kingdom. Now, in a surreal twist, I sat next to Nia, trying to remember everything I had done behind her back to get it all up at once.

When did it start? I wondered. Was it in nursing school when I made friendships with men whose morals didn't align with my own, walking in the council of the ungodly? *Be careful not to blame anyone but yourself.* But had I chosen my friends more wisely, I may have prevented myself from behaving in the same friendly manner with my female classmates as they did. *But I had separated myself from them after graduating,* I remembered. *Why didn't I stop?*

After earning my RN license and starting my first ER nursing job in 2012, I naively thought it would mark a new beginning in overcoming my struggle with desiring other women. I believed that the fulfillment of saving lives, making split-second decisions, and the accompanying adrenaline rushes would satisfy my craving for adventure. Initially, these assumptions proved to be true, but within the first year, a different reality hit.

A growing dissatisfaction with my job began to consume me. The line of work I had spent six years studying for confined me to a box of strict protocols, leaving little to no room for creativity. Rarely did I feel like I was making a difference in someone's life; instead, I felt like I was enabling bad habits. This ill-suited profession, coupled with increasing personal responsibilities, led to depression and then to familiar means to treat it.

****

I pulled into the ER's rear parking lot in my blue scrubs, my mind in a depressive fog.

Turn the car around, Sam, I begged myself. *Don't do this to yourself again.*

As I did day after day, I bit the bullet and shuffled my way into the ER, enduring a job I hated for the sake of my family.

"C.Y.A.," Michelene announced as I exited the break room to start my shift. "Cover. Your. Ass." She said as if we forgot what the letters stood for.

"Here we go again," I said. "Another day of trying to avoid a lawsuit."

The day-shift nurse I was replacing warned me about a patient I was taking over. "He's a revolving-door drug seeker," she said. These patients, who faked their symptoms in search of a high, were the bane of the ER staff's existence. However, it wasn't long into being a nurse that I recognized I had no right to condemn them. I'd happily administer the narcotics they came in for. I was just as guilty of drug-seeking as they were. Maybe their pain wasn't as they described it, but there was *something* they were trying to treat.

Before starting my rounds to greet my new patients, I stopped by the medication room to equip my pockets with IV catheters and saline flushes. As I stepped inside, I stumbled backward in surprise, shocked by what I saw.

"I need help over here!" I yelled. A young female colleague of mine was lying motionless on the floor, a syringe clenched in her hand. Upon rushing to her aid, I noticed an empty morphine vial sitting on the counter.

We're more messed up than our patients, I thought as I stirred her awake. Some of us turned to opioids, others to alcohol, while some of us, such as myself, turned to less conspicuous vices to treat our fears and disappointments.

I returned to my desk, torn between sympathy and judgment for my colleague who had been so reckless about diverting medication from her patients. S*he could've at least waited til' she got home.*

As I counted down the final 30 minutes of my shift, I unwittingly followed my colleague's example. While still on the clock, I reached into my chest pocket for my cell phone for a quick hit of my own narcotic of choice.

"When we meeting up again?" I texted.

****

I engaged the car's cruise control, but my life was about to become anything but steady, veering into lanes I had never driven before. I needed more than just my speed to be controlled; I needed someone else in the driver's seat. I called on God.

My feet were planted on the car's floorboard, but spiritually, I began allowing myself to fall backward. I took one final breath in the world of slavery where I had resided for so long. A nauseating wave of terror came over me. In that suspended moment, between the security of my snare and the free fall below, the only thing I could cling to was trusting that I would land into God's invisible arms.

Live in truth, Sam.

"I need to tell you something," I said.

"Okay?" Nia responded casually, her tone revealing how oblivious she was to my sickness.

"You're not going to like it," I began, trying to prepare her for the most painful words a spouse could ever hear. "It's going to upset you a lot."

"Okay?" She said, this time, her voice carrying a tone of concern.

"I'll start with the worst and work my way through."

Nia jerked back in her seat. "What are you talking about?"

The physical world around me seemed to shrink to just the first few feet of road directly in front of our moving car, forcing me to hyper-focus on the immediate present and not a single moment ahead. Everything beyond it was a dangerous blur.

"I went to a massage parlor like four times," I painfully began. *What the heck are you saying?*

"What are massage parlors?" Nia asked.

"Well," I said, "it's a massage place that offers prostitution. I had sex with one of them." Never before had mere words left such a bitter taste in my mouth. I would have preferred to shove a bar of soap down my throat rather than utter another syllable, but it was too late. The biggest spiritual turning point of my life was underway.

"What?!" Nia cried out, completely blindsided.

"It was horrible," I said. "I'm so so sorry."

"When?!" Nia exclaimed.

"While I was a nurse," I replied. "Three or four years ago, I guess."

Nia's mouth dropped open. She was speechless, looking around the car as if suddenly forgetting where she was. My heart ached for the confusion I saw in her eyes.

Is this what dying to yourself is? I wondered. *Or is this murder?*

I was deliberately placing myself and the person I cherished most in harm's way, entrusting our future to God without any knowledge of the outcome or what the future held. I surrendered all my comfort, at the same time stealing my wife's security, blinding believing that there was something better on the other side.

"You cheated on me?" Nia asked.

"I'm so sorry," I repeated.

With one hand squeezing my temples and the other twisting the leather steering wheel forward, I continued cutting through my snare, at the same time stabbing my wife. "I also went to strip clubs a few times with Mitch."

Nia was in full-tilt shock, her eyes staring right through me as I continued to speak.

"All of this was so long ago, cutie," I tried to explain, "It's not who I am anymore."

Nia always assumed my word was good, that my vows to her were unbreakable. The expression on her face showed just how deep that trust ran. She sat speechless and disturbed. I was tempted to stop to give her time to regain her bearings, but I knew I had to continue before I completely lost my nerve. "There's more," I said.

"Oh my gosh," Nia said.

"I met up with Beth, your old co-worker, off and on for a few months," I stammered. "The most we ever did was kiss and hold hands." Every word I uttered felt like an inscription being carved into my gravestone. *I don't deserve to be alive.*

"Are you kidding me?!" Nia yelled.

"I wish I was," I mumbled. "You don't deserve this."

"When?!" Nia demanded.

"Everything I'm telling you happened at some point before we started going to Pillar," I said. I was losing my stomach. The trust fall into God's invisible arms was taking much longer than I had anticipated. When I began my confessions, I thought I was about to drop from the height of a table, but as I continued speaking, it became clear that I was actually several stories off the ground.

"I can't believe this right now," Nia said as if she were talking to someone in the back seat. I wanted to hug her feet. I was not only causing her immense pain but also making her feel fooled. What she wouldn't understand for many months was that she hadn't been the fool at all; rather, I had been a skilled liar who used her best traits against her. I had been living in survival mode within my marriage, doing whatever it took to avoid this exact catastrophic moment.

For several minutes, Nia and I sat in silence, both of us naked and ashamed. In a self-condemning tone, I thought, *I just had to eat the fruit. I couldn't just trust that God knew what he was talking about. Well, here you go; here's your proof that it was poisonous, you moron.*

"What else is there?" Nia muttered, cupping the sides of her head. Her eyes were shut tight, a grimace on her face as if she were preparing to take another stab.

"I also hung out with Tracy." Each word I spoke seemed to pull my attention further away from the road. The struggle to keep us safe while getting my thoughts out was like trying to steer through a storm without wipers. Amidst this mental tug-of-war, I managed to continue. "We met up like four times, maybe for about an hour each time. We never had sex or anything. We just talked."

"What the heck!?" Nia screamed. "Tracy too!?"

"I'm so so sorry, cutie," I said. My tongue was physically beginning to ache. Such vile words had never left my mouth before. Committing the sins was one thing, but speaking them aloud was something else entirely. Then, I remembered a major detail. *Please, God, no more,* I prayed. Then I opened my mouth.

"We kissed one time and held hands once, I think." *Did I really do these things?* Nia and I both thought I was out to protect her, yet there I was, confessing that not only had I jeopardized her safety, but it seemed I was intent on harming her.

"Oh my gosh!" She screamed, clutching her head. "I can't believe what I'm hearing!"

It was as if we were driving through another dimension; neither of us could wrap our minds around what was truly happening. I wanted to see that there was hope in our future, but I couldn't see anything ahead. I struggled to look *through* the windshield instead of directly at it.

"I'm so, so sorry," I repeated, hoping the words would miraculously envelop Nia in a tight, comforting embrace. Nia's eyes were as wide as they were the night our dresser mirror shattered in the darkness of our bedroom when we both thought the other was being murdered.

"What the heck are you even doing right now?!" she screamed as if she were under physical assault.

"I don't know," I replied. "I can't believe it either. I'm so sorry."

With each new truth unveiled, a rope that bound me fell away, bringing my freedom closer into sight. But as these ropes, saturated with my sins, fell away, they weren't landing on the ground. The snare that I created, once my prison, became Nia's.

21
Nightmare Drive

*But I say, walk by the Spirit, and you will not gratify
the desires of the flesh.*
Galatians 5:16

(Nia)

I SAT AS SAM'S helpless passenger, trying to get my heart to catch up with what my ears were hearing. My hands squeezed each other, trying to hold onto something familiar as Sam confessed to cheating on me multiple times, making it painfully clear that I didn't know the man that I had been living with for the past nine years.

It was only one day prior that I convinced myself I had bravely moved past Sam's biggest failure as a husband—signing up for Ashley Madison. Yet there I was, suddenly thrown into a much stronger, more disorienting tornado of confessions.

Before I could even grasp that I was living out my worst nightmare, I had to clear the fog of confusion and understand what Sam was even doing. *Is he trying to tell me that he cheated on me?* It didn't make sense that this Godly man, who was deeply in love with me and his family, could do such repulsive things behind my back. *Doesn't he love us?* The man sitting beside me, speaking such wicked words, had helped shape me into the moral person I had become. He *despised* lies as a teenager.

Then I remembered a time in high school when Sam suddenly broke up with me a day after he expressed his undying love to me. After a romantic day together, he unexpectedly threw me into a similar unknown universe, leaving me in utter shock as he did on the Seattle car ride.

****

His face was a mix of anger and pain, yet he offered no explanation, only stating, "You know what you did. I'm done playing these games."

A day later, Sam and his brothers drove to Florida to visit their father during our school's week-long fall break, deserting me in a state of bewilderment. Suddenly stuck at home with no boyfriend to enjoy my fall break with, I poured out my thoughts and feelings into a detailed four-page, single-spaced letter for Sam.

When school resumed the following week, I approached him as he ate his cafeteria breakfast and handed him the letter.

"Here," I said, extending him a red folder.

"What's this?" He asked he asked with his eyes.

"It's a letter," I said. "I know it's long, but please read it and get back to me."

"Okay," Sam replied emotionless.

I returned to my table of friends and watched from afar as Sam opened the folder. The first, very long paragraph that greeted him was:

> *Hey Sam! Well, I want to start off by saying I'm sorry we couldn't work out, but it's probably better that we broke up because the closer we got, the harder it would've been to let go when you left! But Thursday night at my house, how could you treat me like you were so in love with me and then break up with me the next day?? We had so much fun together, and we were so happy... I wish I knew what went wrong!?!? Please never do this to another girl who loves you...it's so hard to get over someone when you thought y'all were fine, and then BOOM, out of nowhere..it's over... How confusing!! It really makes me feel stupid, too, because that day, all I could think about was how last time we had a short day with a pep rally, I lost you, and this time, I was so lucky to have you, and we were perfectly in love and happier than any couple on earth. I wrote you a*

note to give you to read while you were in Florida; one part said that no other couple would have happiness, love, or success like us because we chose to honor God and let Him control our relationship... Whatever it is that made you not want me anymore is either stupidity or a lie, but oh well. thank you for the changes you helped me make. I'm pretty sure it'll stay this way, but it would really help if we could still talk and read the bible over the phone. You still read a verse out of that box, right?? You better! That song "She Will Be Loved" and the one by Alicia Keys that I gave you keep coming on the radio like crazy. It's starting to annoy me. Sam, I don't know what's going through your head right now, but I know you're insane for thinking I played games. after I already lost you before????

The following school day, Sam approached me and finally explained that he thought I had been staring at another boy during the pep rally to make him jealous. We cleared up the misunderstanding, and a week later, we started dating again.

****

As if trying to convince Sam that what he was telling me couldn't be true, in response to him telling me he had sex with a prostitute, I said, "But you've always been so private about your body and who you'd be sexual with. You saved your virginity for me."

Where was the guy who insisted on having a strong emotional connection with a girl before even sharing a small kiss, let alone his whole body? Allowing another man to see me without clothes on was so beyond anything I would ever let happen that it made it that much more difficult to believe. We were all each other ever knew, and from my understanding, there was no one else we cared to know.

"I know," Sam responded, grabbing his hair. "It was a really horrible experience."

"Is that supposed to make a difference?!" I yelled.

As horrific as the things coming out of Sam's mouth were, I'd soon learn he was confessing things in the exact opposite order of what he had prepared me for. The first several confessions were shocking, but they didn't tear out my heart like the final few did.

He began with the least of his betrayals: massage parlors, strip clubs, parties, and messaging female Facebook friends. He believed the physical affairs with strangers were worse than the emotional affairs with people I knew, with those I dared even to call my friends.

When the names Beth and Tracy came out of his mouth, everything that kept me grounded, which was very little by this point, was shattered. I had nothing to hold onto. It was as if we'd just been in a car accident; there I was, being flung around the interior, desperately trying to find something, anything, to cling to as the car rolled uncontrollably.

"There was a night that I told you I was taking photos in Dallas alone," Sam said as he began another confession. "I was with Beth."

As much as I wanted to block out the words that were coming from his mouth, I felt forced to listen, like something violent was being done to me against my will. I felt powerless against it.

"I'm so so sorry," Sam kept repeating. All I could hear in his apologies was, *this is over.*

His voice, once a sound that made my stomach flutter, now felt like it was coming from a dangerous stranger. I could barely look at him because of how different he suddenly looked to me. It was his loyalty, love, and adoration for me that had always been the most attractive to me, and that was suddenly thrown out the window.

I had tons of questions, wanting more details, but in fear he'd stop revealing the extent of his confessions, I kept the desire to probe to myself. "Is that everything?" The answer to this question would be the one I'd remember the most.

"As far as the big things go, that's it," Sam claimed. "I did flirt with your co-worker Jane a few times, but she never reciprocated." He made this confession as if it was the least of them, but it immediately sent an electrifying jolt through my body.

"What!?" I screamed.

Anger and shock stung me all over. The complete lack of regard for his family, his Christian morals, and now my closest friends pierced me in my deepest parts. I was in love with someone, but who? *Is he back on the dance floor of our wedding day? Is he all the way back in the high school auditorium where we first locked eyes?*

"Get me out of this car!" I demanded.

"Woah, cutie," Sam replied, stunned by my reaction to this one. "Nothing happened."

"I can't believe I was so dumb," I said. "To think that I was ever proud around my friends that I had a fun and friendly husband, and you were just trying to get with them the whole time!"

Before Jane moved away, she was a cherished friend and co-worker of mine. Sam explained that when he stayed at home for several months between graduating from nursing school and landing a job, he had developed a crush on her. My heart was shattered by the news. I thought she and I shared something special. Why hadn't she told me?

After we returned to our Airbnb, we remained in our parked car, where Sam continued to unveil further details of his affairs and infatuations. Throughout it all, he confessed, he had been watching pornography off and on.

As I scanned my brain for memories of interactions with the women Sam named, a moment came back to me like a shove to my chest. One of my friends had tried to warn me. "Sam played with my hair in a flirty way on the drive to dinner yesterday," my friend Emma told me, "I just thought you should know."

The idea of Sam hitting on, let alone touching, a friend of mine inappropriately was preposterous to me. I immediately assumed she was lying or, at the very least, exaggerating. I didn't talk to her for several weeks because of it.

Feeling the urge to slap Sam building up inside me, I got out of the car before I could give in.

My mind was racing, overwhelmed with every emotion. I loved Sam. *Could our story really end like this?* I wondered. Memories flooded in. Our children's faces, all the love letters exchanged, our wedding day, our nightly prayers, the laughter that filled our home. Was it really going to end so ugly?

I took notice of the scene in front of me as I walked down the middle of the blacktop country road outside our Airbnb. The road was long, dark, and narrow, with little color in sight. Was this the lonely road that my life was headed down? I had always been so supportive of Sam, showing an excessive amount of interest in his dreams, hobbies, and educational pursuits. What had it all been for? Why hadn't I been enough?

After ten minutes to myself, I returned to the car to find Sam in tears. The remorse I saw in him helped me to remain calm as I started questioning him more about his entanglement with Tracy, the one he claimed to have kissed once. I had already distrusted this girl, but suddenly, I found myself hating her with every fiber of my being.

"I told you once that something felt off with our kiss," I began.

"You actually remember that?" Sam asked.

"Were you with her that day!?" I snapped.

"Yes," Sam said.

"I knew it," I said, trying my best once again not to slap him.

There were a number of confessions Sam made that apparently occurred during times that I had been suspicious. I felt angry at myself for pushing aside what I believed to be the Holy Spirit, nudging me to seek answers from my husband. My anger towards Sam became about his allowing me, his committed and faithful wife, to believe the lie that my intuitions were nothing more than paranoia.

"How dare you," I said, shaking my head as I looked into his eyes.

"I'm so sorry, cutie," Sam said.

"Don't you ever call me cutie again," I demanded. "Go tell that to one of your skanky girlfriends."

Once back in the house, I called my best friend, Sandy, and poured out everything that had happened. She was furious on my behalf. We began searching through Sam's Facebook profile to piece together dates, faces, and confessions. It wasn't long before we came across an album of photos from his night out with Beth in Dallas. The discovery brought Sandy and me to tears. By the end of our phone call, my decision was firm: I was divorcing Sam.

22

Unsnared

*The iniquities of the wicked ensnare him,
and he is held fast in the cords of his sin.*
Proverbs 5:22

(Sam)

"HEY GUYS, TODAY has been one of the hardest days of mine and Nia's life by far, especially for Nia," I said into our Canon G7X.

After a tumultuous evening at our Airbnb, one that drove away our friends staying in the next room, I stepped outside to announce to our YouTube audience that we'd be taking an indefinite break from posting. I was vague about why, merely stating that we were going through a difficult season.

"Thanks for being patient with us during this really rough time in our life, but we'll be back," I said, closing out the vlog.

As I lay on the floor in a puddle of regret beside the bed where Nia lay sniffling, it felt like we had each been set adrift in separate boats, oceans apart from each other. I agonized over being the man who severed Nia's anchor line, leaving her to navigate unknown waters alone.

I robbed each of us of our biggest support system. Nia, barely able to shoulder the weight of learning this monstrous side of me, deemed me completely untrustworthy of leading her. As for myself, it goes without saying that I no longer had my wife's respect, let alone her comfort and support. What we still had, however, was our brothers and sisters in Christ giving us their full love and support.

Just a year and a half prior, Nia and I found a church of Christians who immediately surrounded our family, inserting themselves into our lives unlike anyone before them. Nia quickly found a close-knit sisterhood, and I developed friendships with men that were deeper than I ever thought possible. In fact, one of the most transformative relationships of my life began at Pillar Church. I started thanking God for the day He sent Heath into my life.

****

It was Nia's and my second Sunday visiting The Pillar Church. After the service, Nia and I mingled, meeting new faces, when the worship leader—whose vocal skills had really impressed me—approached us.

"Hey, how's it going? I'm Heath. What's your name?" he said, reaching out with a handshake.

Caught off guard by a man whose life seemed very well put together, making his interest in knowing me all the more nerve-wracking, I stammered, "I'm Sam—Samuel, actually. Either is fine, though. Hi. Nice to meet you."

He asked about my family and profession while our daughters played at our feet. Before going our separate ways, he asked a question that marked the start of one of the most significant moments of my life.

"Do you want to grab coffee sometime?"

Although initially, I felt uncomfortable with his question since I had never been invited out by another man before, I drove home with my family that afternoon, feeling seen and valued in a way that was unfamiliar to me.

Three days later, after a night shift in the ER, Heath and I sat outside a Starbucks and began sharing our lives with one another. The discontent, or void within me that I had tried unsuccessfully to fill with countless indulgences, suddenly felt like it had a bottom to it. This Godly man, accomplished, full of wisdom, and extremely talented, sat with me and took his time to get to know who I was beneath the surface. His motivation was clear; he wanted to be a brother and help me know Jesus better.

I committed myself to his mentorship and started meeting with him once a week, forging a bond that felt tighter than a brother. He helped me identify my strengths, point out my blind spots, and confront the sins and temptations in my life, guiding me toward a life that honored God.

Despite trusting him enough to confide in him about everything—my insecurities, depression, struggles with porn, lust, desiring other women's attention, marital disagreements, and so on—my deepest, darkest secrets, the ones I swore I'd carry to my grave, remained unspoken.

No person or thing would get me to betray the secret vow I had made with myself: that the hedonistic lifestyle I had lived the previous five years behind my family's back would remain between me and God for all of eternity.

****

I realized that God had been drawing Nia and me as a couple closer to other believers and, more importantly, as individuals. It seemed that for the past several years, He had been preparing our hearts to face the biggest battle of our lives.

After cutting myself free from the snare I had entrapped myself in, I found new freedom to approach God. Stripped of pretense, I could confidently present every part of myself to Him and come to Him in a way I didn't even know was possible. I gave it all to Him that night.

My reinvigorated relationship with Him helped me deny the creeping thought that, as the perpetrator, I was somehow powerless to help Nia. There may have been oceans between Nia and me, but I wasn't in my boat alone—nor was Nia. God was at the back of our boats, steering each of us to where we needed to go.

The barrier of my secrets, which had also kept me at a safe distance from Nia, was also gone. I could finally love her by God's definition of the word. This was my opportunity to demonstrate just how much I was willing to sacrifice for my bride.

Now, follow my word, God instructed me after freeing me from my snare, *love and cherish your wife*.

To make it even clearer to me that this monumental moment in my marriage had been perfectly orchestrated by God, I remembered that just ten days before being exposed, I had finally been able to quit my day job as a nurse, a financial decision made possible by our pregnancy announcement video going viral.

My marriage is my new full-time job, isn't it God? I prayed with an amused smile. *I'm ready to start.*

I continued talking to God as if He were my best friend, bonding in a new and deeper way as if we had just had a major breakthrough in our relationship. Eventually, in the early hours of the morning, I drifted into a deep, restful sleep.

23
Calling Jane

Therefore I will not restrain my mouth; I will speak in the anguish of my spirit; I will complain in the bitterness of my soul.
Job 7:11

(Nia)

EARLY THE FOLLOWING day, before Sam woke up, after wanting all night to talk to my old friend Jane to get her side of the story, I stumbled out to the backyard and settled into a chair at the firepit, propping my feet up on the stone rim.

I nervously pulled up Jane's Facebook profile on my phone and started typing a short message to her. "You're a good friend. Thank you for not betraying me years ago." I hit send.

According to Sam, Jane never responded to his advances. I was thankful for that, but I was still curious about why she had never told me about it. I hoped my short message would open up that conversation.

As I sat biting at my fingernails, wondering how crazy it was that my life had changed so drastically in an instant, the familiar notification ding from my phone broke my concentration. It was from Jane.

My thoughts paced back and forth as I tried to find the courage to open her message, on the verge of either learning more traumatic details or getting into an argument with a friend I loved and missed so much.

Finally, I tapped it open. "Hey Nia, can we FaceTime?"

This will be interesting, I thought. I hadn't spoken to her since she abruptly moved away and disappeared from my life five years earlier, and now my husband's infidelity would be the reason we connected again.

"Hi, Nia!" She exclaimed. "I've missed you so much!" Her face triggered a rush of memories.

"I've missed *you!*" I exclaimed back, holding back tears.

"I'm so sorry about everything you're going through." She said, referring to the public exposure of Sam's Ashley Madison account.

"Thank you," I said.

"How are you doing?" She asked.

"Well," I began, "Sam just shared *a lot* more with me, including that he pursued you while we were working together, but you never responded to him. I just want to say thank you for that."

"I'm so sorry I never told you," she said. "I assumed I was the only one and thought distancing myself from y'all would make it go away."

"*That's* why you moved away!?" I nearly shouted, tears immediately leaping from my eyes.

"It was a big part of my decision," she said, wiping her eyes. "I really wasn't trying to keep a secret from you, I promise. I love you so much. I just didn't want to disrupt your marriage."

"I believe you," I said, wiping my eyes. "And I don't blame you at all."

Her explanation hit me like a sudden avalanche, and by the end of our call, we found ourselves both sobbing as we revisited our shared past and mourned the loss of our friendship. The same abandoned emotions I had experienced when she moved away came flooding back, but they were now attached to a different person: my husband. I thought Jane had become uninterested in me or, at the very least, indifferent, and that's why she stopped communicating with me. To learn it had been due to my husband's selfish decisions made the pain run even deeper.

After saying our final goodbyes and getting the closure I had always needed, I became furious inside. I was determined to discover more details of Sam's other confessions. I needed to know as much as possible as I tried to fully grasp what had been happening right under my nose. I needed to know how much of my marriage had been fake.

Once again, I meticulously combed through his Facebook activity, scrutinizing everything that fell within the timeframe of his confessions, determined to discover something he wasn't telling me. As I carefully searched for clues of his infidelity in every photo, knowing full well Sam's poetic nature and inability to keep his emotions to himself, I came across a comment he made to a girl that I had once confronted him about.

Shaking my head in frustration, I suddenly recalled a long-forgotten memory from the second year of our marriage. It had me asking myself once again, *why didn't I just trust myself?*

****

Before Sam returned home from a day at nursing school, I enlarged a Facebook comment feed on his computer screen. In it, he had made two comments to a female nursing classmate that I found inappropriate: one complimenting her smarts and the other expressing that he missed her over their break.

"Okay?" Sam said as he sat down at his computer, already claiming his innocence. "What's your point?"

"We agreed that we wouldn't add the opposite sex on Facebook," I replied. "This is exactly why."

"Why, so I can't communicate with my classmates?" Sam sarcastically asked.

"No. So we can protect our marriage!" I exclaimed.

"First off, I don't find this girl attractive at all," He said. "Second, I'm just being friendly."

"That's totally beside the point!" I shouted.

We went back and forth, arguing whether or not what he said to the girl was flirting. Sam argued that he didn't want to isolate himself from his classmates. I tried to explain that complimenting other women felt like a betrayal. Our argument moved from a mostly civilized exchange of words to outright trying to outscream each other. Sam finally left the room, leaving me crying, with one last spiteful threat: "If you really want me to give you something to be jealous about, I will!"

We made up that night, as we usually did, with Sam agreeing to take his online friendliness down a notch. However, this didn't change the fact that he would be going back to school the following day to spend more time with other women than time with me, and it wouldn't take away the suspicions that had me questioning him, to begin with.

****

Then, I came across another photo that caught my attention and nearly made my heart stop. It was a photo that Sam took of me and our children alongside Tracy and her children, the girl I had always distrusted, during an outing we had together at a waterpark. She had tagged Sam and me in the photo, even though Sam wasn't even in it.

Looking at a photo of this woman in her bathing suit, standing right next to me, unexpectedly brought color to Sam's infidelity in a whole new, painful way. It tore at my very core.

My whole life seemed like nothing but a big lie. I broke out in a sweat. My hands and legs felt weak and shaky as I came to the realization that this woman and my husband had been on a date right under my nose. I stormed back into the house.

24
Self-Mutilation

*He who commits adultery lacks sense;
he who does it destroys himself.
Proverbs 6:32*

(Sam)

"OW!" WAS THE first sound I uttered the following morning.

I sat up, discovering a hairbrush had been thrown at my head. There stood Nia in the doorway of our room, giving me a deep, terrifying glare.

"You hit on Jane and actually thought she'd respond to a scumbag like you!?" Nia shouted.

It was a valid question, but in my dazed state, I was at a loss for words. "I don't know," I mumbled, my head drooping in a blend of sleepiness and shame.

Sleep was not just my greatest pleasure; it was essential for my equilibrium, more so than the average person, and I had barely managed to get half a night's rest. My flesh wanted to roll back up in my blanket and get my ten hours of sleep as usual, but the conversation God and I had the night before was fresh on my mind.

Adjusting to Nia's early morning routine and ensuring I was fully available to her was the first major challenge in this new fight for my

Self-Mutilation

marriage. Mornings would serve as a litmus test, revealing not only to Nia but also to myself the depth of my remorse and commitment to making things right again. That morning, I said goodbye to the luxury of a full night's rest.

"I'm so sorry," I muttered, rubbing my forehead as I rose to sit on the bed.

"Answer me," Nia demanded. "Did you really think a Godly woman like Jane would respond to you?"

"I don't know," I said, "but yeah, I guess so."

"You're disgusting," Nia concluded. "She's way too good for you."

I nodded my head.

"She just cried to me on the phone and told me she moved away because of *you*!" Nia shouted. "You're a sorry human being."

I'd be lying if I said I wasn't afraid of what Nia might do next, knowing I deserved much more than a brush to the head. I sat there, eyes closed, resting my head on my fingertips, disgusted that I had been the reason Nia lost a friend. *Where do I go from here, God?* I prayed. *This doesn't seem fixable.*

"Pack up our stuff!" Nia demanded before leaving the room and slamming the door shut.

It was a painfully heavy moment to learn that a friendship was ruined and a person moved away all due to my lack of self-control. The consequences of my behavior extended far beyond my own home. In my pursuit to take from others what I thought was lacking in myself, I overlooked not only my wife's feelings but also those of the other women I targeted.

Recollections of other times when my reckless actions probably hurt others, and not just Nia, started to resurface. One, in particular, came back clearly and painfully. My heart started pounding when I realized it was a betrayal that I hadn't yet told Nia about. *I can't do this to her again.*

****

After finally alleviating my patient's internal torment with an anti-anxiety injection, I pulled up a chair and sat at her bedside. As I watched her slowly doze off, her cut wrists tied down to the bed frame, I couldn't help but relate to her.

As of late, my decisions had seemed nothing less than a form of self-mutilation. I never reached the point of suicidal ideation as she had, but my vice was just another way to feel something other than the depression and discontent that engulfed me. The choice I was minutes away from making, however, would jeopardize the world as I knew it and might as well have been called suicide.

Once my patient started snoring, I left her room and fell into my desk chair. It had been an exhausting night, moving patients in and out of the ER like I was herding cattle rather than helping humans. Moments earlier, I was frantically unwrapping monitor cables from around my patient's neck, a failed attempt at strangling herself, in the process pulling a muscle in my back.

Desperate to escape my sympathy-sucking environment, I opened Craigslist on my phone, but regretfully, it wasn't for a session of retail therapy. I navigated to the "Men Searching for Women" section.

As I scrolled through a list of mostly advertisements for pornographic sites, a particular listing mid-way down the page caught my attention. I tapped on it. The description challenged men to "prove" they were "man enough," rounded off with a cheeky, "Good luck, cowboys." Intrigued, I crafted a short response, offering up my first name and best qualities.

Within minutes, my phone notified me of a new email: It was from her. I tapped on it. Her reply read, "Can you send me a photo?" As with other sites I ventured on, I had expected my email to drown in a sea of countless responses from other wayward men.

I hesitated, my finger hovering over my phone's screen. *What if she recognizes me?* I thought. I felt there was a small risk of being identified, especially since Nia had numerous connections in our area, but in my reckless mindset, I pushed aside my apprehension; besides, it was these kinds of gambles that gave me the thrill I was seeking.

I attached a photo of myself and hit send.

The email that blinked back sent the worst kind of chills down my spine. "Omg! I know who you are!" It read. "I feel so bad for Nia!"

"Oh my gosh!" I exclaimed aloud, nearly falling backward in my chair. My words echoed through the quiet ER.

"Are you okay?" A nurse friend chuckled from the other end of the nurse's station.

"Yeah, I'm fine," I laughed. "Just making sure you guys are awake."

A wave of dizziness washed over me. My stomach churned with queasiness as my mind raced with images of Nia at home in our bed, receiving a message from this person, exposing me for everything I was. "Look what your husband's been up to," I imagined her text reading. The pain I imagined coming over Nia's face made me want to die.

I sank into my chair, buried my face in my hands, and whispered, "It's over."

With trembling fingers, I composed my next email, "OMG, I'm so sorry! I was just messing around out of boredom at work. I have no intention of ever cheating on Nia." Attempting to redirect the conversation, I added, "How do you know her?"

She replied, "You both know me. I went to school with y'all."

Desperate to make her feel like a guilty accomplice in my straying, thus reducing the likelihood of her telling anyone, I attempted to keep the conversation moving. "What a humiliating coincidence this is. I'm just looking to have a friendly chat with someone. That's all, I swear. So, who are you?"

"I'm too embarrassed to say," came her quick reply, the situation seemingly swinging in my direction.

I replied, "I promise you my embarrassment is plenty for both of us. Now I really have to know."

"Samantha White." She replied.

When I read her name, I felt so embarrassed I could puke. Nia and I had indeed shared high school hallways with this girl. To compound the awkward situation, she worked at a restaurant that our family frequented often. She always welcomed each of us with warm, southern-style hugs and seemed to develop a special affection for the very family she caught me betraying.

I took some comfort in recalling that even though she was mostly overlooked in high school, I had always treated her kindly and was intentional about making her feel seen. Based on what I thought I knew about her, it seemed my secret would be safe with her.

By the end of our conversation, I assured her that Nia was in good hands, and she agreed to keep our exchange between us.

I stacked my life-risking decision on top of an already massive mound of shame and, as usual, vowed never to speak of it again.

The familiar side hugs with Samantha continued, but now they carried a painfully awkward, silent undertone that only she and I understood.

****

My Craigslist secret, which I had nearly forgotten about, troubled me more deeply than ever. It was the moment I realized that my confessions to Nia were far from over.

My heart pounded. *Please, God, no, not again,* I pleaded. It was beyond my comprehension how I could ever repeat the traumatic event of our previous day's car ride. "I can't tell her another one," I whispered to myself, panic building inside me. "There's no way."

Over the following several weeks, I'd learn that my bigger betrayals were like boulders resting on many other smaller rocks—numerous, less memorable betrayals. Then, beneath these, more stones lay hidden —the painful details of my affairs, such as locations and things said. I was faced with the reality that each one of these stones would have to be thrown at my wife by none other than her very husband. The entirety of my confessions would be agonizingly drip-fed to Nia, resetting the clock after each one was revealed.

PART 5
Mirages and Mana
The aftermath of confession

25
Missed Flight

The Lord is close to the brokenhearted;
he rescues those whose spirits are crushed.
Psalms 34:18

(Nia)

MY FRUSTRATIONS PEAKED when, at 10 PM, despite Sam and I sprinting to our designated airport gate, we were met by a shut door and a boarding agent who refused to let us through.

"Please!" I begged. "Tomorrow is my daughter's first day of kindergarten!"

"Ma'am," Sam said, "people are literally still boarding the plane."

"Sorry, it's policy," the agent replied.

Not only was my marriage falling apart before my eyes, but now I wouldn't be present for one of the most important days of my child's life. I was fuming inside. I had pre-planned everything before our trip to ensure the special day went as smoothly for Symphony as possible, and now it was all out of my control.

Usually, Sam would have us waiting at the gate at least two hours before take-off, but this time, he misjudged several things, getting us to our gate five minutes after boarding time ended. Although I was reluctant to continue relying on him, exchanging as few words as necessary, I demanded that he do everything possible to get me home in time to take my firstborn child to her first day of school.

Standing there, watching Sam's weary, desperate, and apologetic face as he spoke with an airline agent, trying to get us another flight, I recognized how his failure in getting us to our gate on time felt a lot like the confessions he had made to me the previous day. Both left me feeling abandoned and like I could never count on him again. My doubts about his ability to make things right in our marriage were intensified. My situation seemed more hopeless than ever.

In what appeared to be the start of him keeping his promise to do whatever it took, Sam paid a crazy amount for seats on another flight. This would get us to Dallas at 5 AM and hopefully back home by 7 AM.

Both of our mothers were at our house when we arrived in the nick of time at 7:15 AM. This was the first time they had seen us since the news of Sam's Ashley Madison account broke the internet. Upon entering, neither said anything more than "hello" to Sam.

I went straight to Symphony's room, doing everything I could to be completely present with her while saying as little to her dad as possible. Symphony's beauty and innocence offered me a brief mental and emotional respite as I scooped her up, held her in my arms, and dressed her in her little school uniform.

"You look so precious," I said to Symphony before kissing her cheeks.

As much as I wanted to tell Sam to leave the house, for Symphony's sake, I kept quiet and allowed her to have her daddy present until she went to school. Besides, it brought me satisfaction that Sam had to be around my mom after such terrible revelations about him had come to light. My mom adored Sam and thought the world of him and vice versa. The weight and embarrassment he would undoubtedly feel while being around her was enough punishment for the moment.

As I brushed Symphony's hair, I overheard Sam asking each of our moms if he could speak privately with them. Although my mom only knew the tip of the iceberg of Sam's betrayals, I could hear in her voice that she was hurting for me.

Wise enough to know there was more to the story, she said, "I've seen what happens to families when they go down this path, Sam. It's full of destruction." She took on the role of my caring mom and protective dad. I loved every word I heard and treasured her all the more for it.

Upon arriving at the Christian school where Symphony would attend, I met Sandy and her son, who was also starting Kindergarten, in the school courtyard. Sam followed us with his camera, capturing one of my life's most confusing and emotional days. A month later, he uploaded it to our channel with the title *Emotional First Day Of School*.

I took pictures of Sandy and her son, and she took pictures of Symphony and me. Sam wanted a photo of the three of us together, but I refused. Reluctantly, and only for Symphony's sake, I took a photo of Sam and her together.

I looked him square in the eyes and said, "I'm done taking pictures with you. Get used to it."

I turned my focus back to Symphony and her classmates and watched them walk in single file under a beautifully shaded path lined with flowers. In the distance, a group of teenagers laughed and kicked a ball around in an open field as if life was good. I determined right then that this day would be the beginning of a new chapter for me.

As Sam walked back to our car in tears, I headed straight for the office and volunteered for recess, lunch, and parking lot duty. I was set on showing Sam and myself that I would move on without him, not allowing his selfishness to unmotivate me. I had allowed him to witness enough heartbreak in me.

Back in the parking lot, Sandy and I cried together after having sent our firstborn children off to school for the first time. It seemed like yesterday that we had fulfilled our high school dreams of becoming mothers together, and we were saying goodbye in what seemed like the snap of a finger.

When I returned to my car, Sam was still in tears, sitting in the driver's seat. "Let's go," I said, emotionless.

We were scheduled to meet with Pastor Bo and Chantel at our church building later that day. Sam and I had different reasons for agreeing to this meeting, however. Sam's intention, or so I thought, was to start the process of putting our marriage back together, while mine was to ensure that our pastors knew every single sleazy detail of Sam's past and to get their blessing for me to leave him.

26
Life Sentence

*The instruction of the wise is like a life-giving fountain;
those who accept it avoid the snares of death.*
Proverbs 13:14

(Sam)

JUST AFTER PULLING away from our small blue brick house, I came to a rolling stop to greet an elderly neighbor, a friend of ours, who was checking her mailbox.

"Hi Peg," I said through my passenger-side window. "It's a beautiful day to be checking the mail."

During a casual exchange about the weather, she paused mid-sentence and abruptly said, "I just want you to know that I saw you in People magazine, accused of being on that site, but I don't believe a word of it."

I knew exactly what she was referring to. Nia had come across the same article while waiting in line at our local grocery store. The subtitle read, "Josh Duggar wasn't the only popular young religious figure to have his secrets outed by the Ashley Madison hackers."

Despite being flushed with embarrassment, I admitted to Peg that the accusations were indeed true and that I was currently on my way to meeting Nia for another marriage counseling session.

"Well," she began thoughtfully, "If each of you strives to move closer to Jesus, your paths will inevitably meet back up at the common ground of His name."

Her unexpected wisdom boosted my sense of hope, helping prepare my heart for the emotionally exhausting day that awaited me. If Nia and I continued to anchor our lives in Jesus, the master of redemption, we'd naturally meet back up at reconciliation.

God, please draw me and Nia closer to you.

Our counseling session with Bo and Chantel kicked off with the usual friendly banter. It was our second sit-down with them. Our first meeting occurred the day before, during which Nia and I brought Bo and Chantel up to speed on everything. We had also arranged for me to start staying in their guest bedroom while Nia decided whether or not she wanted to stay married to me.

At an opportune pause in our banter, Bo slapped his armrests and said, "Okay, let's pray and jump in."

After his prayer, Bo turned to me and asked, "Have you had any new revelations?"

My heart pounded.

Continuing to open up about my past to Nia turned out to be remarkably similar to my lifelong aversion to vomiting. Although I knew that purging would ultimately make me feel better, the process felt too unnatural not to resist. I'd always do everything in my power to hold it down. In both cases, I struggled with the fear of the momentary acidic sting, even when I knew that release would bring relief.

"I don't think it's helping anyone to keep giving more details," I said, "and having to keep starting back at square one."

"Awesome, you're still keeping secrets," Nia said sarcastically, shaking her head as anger painted her face.

"I just feel like we're bringing back to life things that are long gone and dead now," I argued.

Bo looked into my eyes. "Nia deserves to know exactly what it is she's going to need to forgive and move past before she begins to do so, Sam."

"It's just so cruel," I muttered, breaking out in a sweat as the moment drew nearer.

"Aww, poor little ol' Sammy is uncomfortable," Nia said, her voice dripping with disdain. "You have no clue how cruel this is! I'll be the one to determine that thank you. Now tell me!"

"Sam," Chantel began, "Nia is still assessing the damage and trying to decide if rebuilding trust in your marriage is possible. You need to give her as much as she wants to know."

"Remember, Sam," Bo added, "live in truth. Bring it all into the light so both of you can walk out of the darkness."

I knew Bo was right. My secrets and the truth were incompatible. They couldn't coexist in me anymore. I used to be a nurse; I knew better. Expelling my secrets would relieve the debilitating nausea that was my guilt and remove the toxins that were my shame. Vomiting is a protective reflex, and I needed to stop fighting God's design and get it all up before it led to more severe health issues. I opened my mouth and surrendered.

"There was a night during nursing school when I told you I was going to go see a movie with Mitch. I actually went to a strip club." I paused to catch my breath. "I took my wedding ring off that night and kept it in my shoe."

Nia looked at me, her breathing increasing and her eyes narrowing. "Wow," she said. "You wanted this marriage over long before I did." Then she yelled, "Why didn't you just leave me and spare me all this!?"

"Because I never wanted to leave you," I said.

"Yeah, yeah, whatever," Nia said. "What else?"

"There was a night I went out with my brother and Aaron, and I told you we stayed the night in a hotel," I started.

"And?" Nia asked.

"We never slept at the hotel. We took photos at it to make it look like we did. We drank and went to clubs." The room was silent except for Nia's heavy, angry breathing.

Nia finally responded, "Were you *trying* to pay me back for something?" Nia looked at Chantel, "Not only was he chasing after my friends right under my nose, but he was playing tricks on me too. He was clearly trying to get me back for something!"

"Of course not," I replied. "You did absolutely nothing wrong. I was just trying to hide it from you so I wouldn't lose you."

"I don't believe you," Nia replied. "And guess what? You *are* going to lose me."

"I don't think Sam did any of this out of revenge for anything you did or didn't do, Nia," Bo said. "From what I know about Sam and from what I've learned about infidelity in general, I think Sam did most of these things from a place of low self-esteem."

I nodded my head in agreement, thankful for Bo's insightful explanation.

He continued, "Other women being attracted to him probably built up his self-confidence momentarily and made him feel better than he did about himself. I think those were the feelings he was mostly chasing."

What Bo said opened my eyes to something I had never fully acknowledged. It had been a lifelong habit of mine to find any reason to self-deprecate or berate myself. It was a very rare occasion that I felt worthy around others. Much of my extramarital behavior was likely an attempt to bury feelings of inadequacy or to replace insecurities with external validation, pointing to a lack of understanding of what my true identity in Christ was.

"Okay," Nia said, "what about him chasing after my friends?"

"Affairs usually occur with someone known to both partners, such as a friend, coworker, or neighbor," Bo continued. "What Sam did is absolutely a deeper kind of betrayal, but it's not uncommon in adultery."

"Is there anything else you've remembered, Sam?" Chantel asked.

I pinched the bridge of my nose and closed my eyes, then told Nia about coming across Samantha on Craigslist and other brief conversations with women on the site that never amounted to anything but words exchanged.

Nia laughed mockingly, shaking her head as if she had never seen a bigger idiot than me. "I bet that was real fun being caught cheating by someone who loves your family so much," she said.

"Anything else, Sam?" Bo asked.

I continued to confess more inappropriate interactions with women: messages sent, comments made, and moments of being alone with other women, such as the time I sat with a co-worker alone in her car for a few minutes before our shift began. I gave in without a fight to anything that wanted to come up, no matter the size.

I had underestimated the amount of poison I was infected with. The more I opened my mouth, the more I felt I didn't deserve forgiveness. I traded fleeting moments of carnal pleasure, forgettable and profoundly unsatisfying, for what promised to be years, if not a lifetime, of pain in my wife's heart and the burden of cleaning up the huge mess I left in my wake.

By the end of our counseling session, I felt no less than a criminal deserving of a life sentence. The things I had done were nothing less than murderous. Yet, it seemed it would be Nia who would bear the weight of my punishment. It sickened me to the core.

What did I do? I asked myself. I resisted the urge to berate myself or entertain thoughts of defeat and inadequacy. *You're not allowed to mope,* I told myself. *Look at your wife! Who cares what you think about yourself!?* I became more determined than ever to be available to Nia as humanly possible. She deserved nothing but the very best I had to give.

The next several weeks would be my biggest test of perseverance as I strived to meet Nia at Jesus's feet. However, as I navigated the path of redemption, I didn't consider there'd be other unique battles we'd face along the way, such as surprise temptations and unwise spontaneous choices.

27
Redhead at Walmart

*Never avenge yourselves, but leave it to the wrath of God,
for it is written, "Vengeance is mine, I will repay, says the Lord."
Romans 12:19*

(Nia)

"GOD, WHY!?" I screamed, beating my fist on the steering wheel.

I was headed home after volunteering for recess at Symphony's school. I was crying so hard that the tears blurred my vision, causing me to swerve dangerously on the road.

I pulled into our driveway and sat, struggling to comprehend how my happy marriage had suddenly turned into something I hated. Just last week, we were seemingly deeply in love.

I took a lot of pride in my husband. I admired how he could make the perfect joke at the perfect time to make anyone feel comfortable in our presence. The very qualities I loved most about him seemed to be the source of the greatest pain of my entire life as if they had been out to trick me all along.

As I angrily replayed what little Sam told me regarding the things he and other women talked about, my imagination ran wild. I hit the steering wheel again. Then, *Fight Song* by Rachel Platten started playing on the radio.

I turned the volume all the way up, trying to drown out the vengeful thoughts in my head. I sang the words as loud as I could, "This is my fight song, take-back-my-life song, prove-I'm-alright song," hoping I could somehow make them true for myself. But still, the only fight I could visualize involved pulling a particular person's hair and dragging her around by it.

I sat thinking about what my next move should be. Agreeing to stay with Sam and work on our broken marriage seemed not only a confession of weakness—that I couldn't do life without him—but also as if I were condoning his cheating. If I didn't punish him for the pain he had caused me, who would? But then, if I did go my separate way, would it be a mere distrust in God that caused me to give up? I felt torn between wanting to throw it all away and not allowing evil to win.

I jumped out of the car, in a hurry to start a new life, one way or another. If I couldn't erase what Sam did, I would wipe away any evidence of his betrayals left behind in my house. I first threw out his favorite pair of shoes, brown leather slip-ons that he wore everywhere, apparently even to strip clubs. I discarded shirts, sweaters, and pants, anything that remotely reminded me of the Sam in the early years of our marriage.

As I sifted through his closet in search of his old blue nursing scrubs, ready to tear them up and trash them, a jealous moment that occurred while I was running an errand for Sam came flooding back into my memory.

****

I sped into the Walmart parking lot, slammed the gear into park, and walked briskly past the grocery carts and into the store. I had 15 minutes while Sam was at home getting ready for work to grab him a Mexican food item to take with him. I grabbed some tortilla chips and headed to the produce section for fresh salsa.

If the lines are short, I could be out of her with five minutes to spare, I thought.

After my hand swooped down to grab the salsa, I spun around to head for the cash register but was compelled to suddenly stop when I saw Sam's co-worker heading down the shopping aisle towards me.

"Hey!" I exclaimed.

It was imperative that this woman saw me in my prime "super-wife" mode. I offered my biggest, brightest smile as red hair against blue scrubs approached me. My snap decision was to pretend we knew each other. In reality, she was nothing more than my husband's attractive colleague.

"Hey!" She responded.

"It's so good to see you!" I said. "I guess you're getting food for the potluck?"

"Yeah," she responded. "I see Sam sent you out to pick up his part." She laughed.

"Yep," I said. "So when you guys are eating chips and salsa tonight, just know I made it possible." We shared a loud and overly hearty laugh as I held up the items.

"Well, I hope you guys have a fun dinner tonight," I added.

"Oh, we will," she responded. "Sam is hilarious. You must be laughing all the time."

Thrown off guard by a stab of jealousy, I muttered, "Definitely. That boy is crazy."

After an awkward moment of silence, we exchanged farewells and went our separate ways. Once I got back to my car, the fake smile disappeared.

No matter the relationship, I hated sharing Sam with other women. Trying to find a silver lining to make myself feel better, I remembered how well-dressed I was. *At least I was put together,* I thought.

When I arrived back home, I sent Sam off with his items and, as usual, a love note inside. I fed my children dinner, straightened up the house, and then jumped into bed. Snuggled up to my body pillow in one of Sam's shirts, I kept replaying my interaction with the redhead at Walmart.

I had told her that Sam and I laughed all the time together. The truth was, however, that was how it used to be. Lately, when he was home, he seemed emotionally distant and irritable. He told me it was due to working the night shift and his "circadian rhythm" being "disrupted." But I wondered if, in reality, Sam was living two separate lives. Before my imagination got the best of me, I fell asleep, praying for God to fix whatever was going wrong and help my marriage return to normal.

****

Closing up the black trash bag of Sam's belongings felt immensely satisfying, almost as if I was beginning to walk on the path of acceptance. But after replaying the Wal-Mart memory, anger came flooding back. I threw the bag in the garbage bin and hated that I had ignored my intuition so many times. I wanted to throw even more out, like Sam's wedding vows to me. I took off my wedding ring, resisting the urge to flush it down the toilet, and threw it into my jewelry box.

After getting into our bed alone, I remembered that on the nights leading up to Sam's confessions, we had been watching the show *Friday Night Lights* together. We'd snack and cuddle close, appreciating the fact that we'd never have to say goodbye, just as we always dreamed. I remembered how he had reacted to a scene of unfaithfulness in the show. He was disgusted by it. *Was he thinking about himself?* I wondered. I drifted off to sleep, trying not to cry as I came to terms with the fact the best part of my day had suddenly been yanked out of my life.

I woke up the next morning still feeling empty inside but able to see my situation a little more realistically. I played *Fight Song* again and put it on repeat as I made breakfast.

I was beginning to realize that staying with Sam would be much harder than leaving him. Sure, starting a new life without him would be a struggle involving becoming independent, finding a job, etc, but if I were looking for a real fight, it would come from staying with Sam.

Taking the road of least resistance was never something God had ever asked of me. Despite my pain and confusion, I was sensible enough to know that although I wasn't aware of the details, God had a plan for me. Whatever it was, I knew I didn't want to miss out on it, no matter what was required of me to get there.

Thankfully, I was surrounded by several women of God who regularly checked in on me, encouraging me not to let anger be the filter through which I viewed my marriage and Sam. They tried to balance my negative thoughts by reminding me to look at the bright side of my situation, namely that Sam was doing everything in his power to show how apologetic he was and that he was a changed man.

I agreed to keep going to marriage counseling, listening to what this man who had turned my world upside down had to say for himself. Had I been warned about the mistakes I was vulnerable to making, however, I would have stayed as far away from Sam as possible until my intense and unpredictable emotions settled down.

28

The Guardrail

A man without self-control is like a city broken into and left without walls.
Proverbs 25:28

(Sam)

"...AND LORD, THANK you for small victories. Amen." After Pastor Bo finished his opening prayer for our fourth marriage counseling session, he said, "Okay, Sam, let's talk about what specific things Nia needs from you now. What do you think that is?"

After a short pause, I turned to Nia and said, "I think she needs me to show her the guardrails I've put up in our marriage and will continue to put up to make sure these things never happen again."

"Good answer!" Chantel laughed in a deep, hearty chuckle.

"Tell us more about that, Sam," Bo said with a smile.

I had been thinking a lot about roadway guardrails recently and their significance in my life. Guardrails are put in very specific places for a very specific purpose: to save drivers from notoriously dangerous areas.

For the sake of not only my marriage but also my relationship with God, I needed to reflect deeply on my past mistakes, identify the danger areas, and put up guardrails in those places before getting back

The Guardrail

on the road.

I remember my oldest brother, Matthew, sharing his thoughts on our dad's infidelity. He said, "Dad modeled for us that the boundary of adultery isn't just crossable—he showed us exactly how valuable it was to him and what he was willing to sacrifice for it." I couldn't help but wonder how things might have been different for us if Dad had instead emphasized the importance of guardrails in marriage and had gone to equally great lengths to avoid crossing them.

It's a strange coincidence that both Matthew and I owe our lives to the meticulous attention given to the construction and location of guardrails on our roads, yet it seems we owe our biggest failures to our father's lack of such attention.

"It's interesting because I've seen the significance of the presence *and* absence of guardrails," I uttered, my poetic side coming out as the most terrifying moment of my life flashed before my eyes.

****

It was a warm winter afternoon in December 2007, a year before I would propose to Nia. I stood next to a Texas state trooper, tears in my eyes, recounting the traumatic events that had just unfolded when Nia swung her car into a screeching U-turn, pulling onto the shoulder. She burst from her car and threw her arms around my neck. "I'm so glad you're alive," she whispered.

I had been driving my newly purchased 1998 Toyota Corolla as my brother Matthew worked on a Sudoku puzzle in the passenger seat on a stretch of highway I had driven countless times before. We were headed into town to grab a Blizzard together.

My speedometer hovered around 65 MPH as I pulled out my Nokia flip phone. Predictive texting allowed me to believe I could multitask, i.e., text and drive. Without taking my eyes off the road, I pressed the digits *4-9-2-6-8-8*, and then briefly looked at the tiny phone screen to verify it had suggested the correct words.

"THUD! THUD! THUD! THUD!"

An abrupt dip diverted both my and Matthew's focus from our distractions. My passenger-side tires were suddenly off the road. I hit the brake pedal and pulled the steering wheel to the left, but my speed and direction remained unchanged. My old tires were on loose dirt and had lost their traction.

I looked up to see we were headed directly toward the end cap of a roadway guardrail called "the terminal." The kind marked by diagonal black and yellow reflector decals. It was the exact terminal that seemed to lock gaze with me each time I passed it. "You can't escape me forever," it would tauntingly whisper. I had always feared that I would die or, worse, become incapacitated from colliding with one of these, and now, my nightmare was on the verge of becoming a reality.

The second before meeting the guardrail, I let out a blood-curdling scream, emptying my lungs of what I was sure would be my last breath, "Noooooooooooo!"

With a deafening crash, the Corolla slammed dead on into the guardrail terminal. The seat belt tightened against my chest as the airbags deployed with a crack and a whoosh. We didn't come to a sudden stop as I had expected. Instead, we gradually slowed down as we plowed deeper into the rail as if it were an oversized spring. Then, we recoiled off it and spun into the grass until the Corolla came to a standstill, facing the opposite direction, just feet away from a steep embankment. My ears rang as I took in a breath of dust particles and smoke.

"Are you okay, bro?!" Matthew asked, his Sudoku puzzle no longer in sight.

"I think so," I said as I looked over my body.

We climbed out of the car, trying to understand how our lives had been spared rather than speared. The guardrail looked like a peeled-back can of sardines. On impact, the car had pushed the terminal into the rail behind it. After years of fearing crashing into this terminal, I learned that I had been believing a lie. It was there to save me, to act as a cushion if I were to hit it, not to claim my life at all.

I sat in the grass behind my totaled Toyota, watching Matthew as he took photos of the wreckage. As I thanked God for our lives, my relief turned into grief. Not only did I lose the $5000 car that I had spent all year saving up for, but I had risked my brother's life to send Nia a text message.

Nia arrived soon after to pick us up. As we drove away, a subtle and comforting thought reassured me that Matthew and I still had unfinished business on this earth—that God wasn't done with us yet. Questions like *Why did I survive something that I was so sure would kill me?* swirled in my mind for months after the wreck. It would be over a decade before I started to understand the true meaning of that day.

****

"What specific guardrails do you think are important?" Bo asked, playing along with my metaphor.

"Well, for one, I wasn't meeting regularly with other Christian men, something I've been doing now," I said. "Meeting regularly with Heath turned my life around, and I've continued to do that."

A few men had drifted in and out of my life, but none had journeyed alongside me as Heath had. He held a compass and map before me, guiding me through a world of temptation and lies, always there to point me to the path of Life.

"This is pointless," Nia interrupted, looking at Chantel. "The list of things I would need to even *remotely* begin to trust him again is too long. It's impossible that he'd ever be able to make me feel safe again."

"I'll do whatever it takes," I responded. "You already have all my passwords and full access to all my social accounts. I'll sync our Apple accounts so you can check my location any time." My love for Nia was finally an open door.

"It's obvious that there weren't many boundaries established when you guys got married," Bo began. "Of course, in large part, that's due to Sam not being open about his struggles. Nia needs to hear as many specifics as possible about how you're going to protect her."

Three hours later, Nia and I were back at home. Although I'd be sleeping in Bo's guest bedroom that night, I accompanied her to the house to help her with nightly routines. After praying with Abram and Symphony, I poured us each a glass of wine and waited for Nia on the couch.

"How do you think tonight went?" I asked as she walked into the room.

"Even if you meant everything you said, I just doubt you'll be able to keep these so-called guardrails up for very long," Nia replied.

I looked into her eyes, "I meant every word I said, and I guarantee that I will always be accountable to other men *and* you for the rest of my life. I've been to prison, and trust me, I'm not going back."

"But you used to say a little flirting was innocent," Nia said, kissing her wine.

"That's not me anymore," I said, "nor has it been in a long time."

"Okay," Nia said, seeming receptive to my pleas.

"I love you so much," I added. "Please remember, too, my relationship with God is deeper and more real than ever."

"Yeah," Nia said, taking another drink of her wine. "Do you think you could ever cheat again, whether it's me or somebody else?" she asked.

"I'll say this," I began, "the moment you see my relationship with God slipping is when we both should fear that I might backslide."

"So you *could* do this again?" Nia asked.

"Unfortunately, probably," I said. "Without Jesus to fulfill me, I've already seen that I'm capable of anything. But that's exactly why we need strict boundaries and open conversations like these regularly. You have no idea how long I've wanted to talk openly with you about these things."

"I hear what you're saying," Nia said, "but that's hard to hear."

After I agreed to more safeguards, such as never drinking alcohol outside of our home, not going into the bathroom alone with my phone, only going out with solid Christian friends, etc., Nia and I continued to have one of the most vulnerable and vital conversations we had ever had.

I leaned in close to her. "I'm so sorry that I did this to us," I said, tears welling up. "You have no idea how thankful I am to be sitting here with you." The mere brush of her nightgown against my skin became a bittersweet reminder of how much I needed her touch.

Nia replied, "I do appreciate you being so open with me." She continued to express regret that I had ever felt unable to confide in her about my inner struggles. She wished I had reached out to her sooner. "I think you underestimated how much I can handle," she added.

Feeling a mix of fear and desperation, I asked, "Can I please kiss you? I really miss you."

After a long pause, her finger tracing the rim of her empty wine glass, she replied, "Okay."

29
One-Night Stand

As soon as he had finished speaking to Saul, the soul of Jonathan was knit to the soul of David, and Jonathan loved him as his own soul.
1 Samuel 18:1

(Nia)

AFTER OUR FOURTH marriage counseling session, during a late-night conversation with Sam over wine, still trying to wrap my mind around my new life, I allowed Sam to kiss me. The kiss turned into making out, which turned into what I called the "one-night stand with my husband."

When the moment ended, I broke down in tears and hurried Sam away, feeling embarrassed and angry. I was upset with myself for being weak enough to give in to him and troubled by the thought that he may have been emotionally manipulating me all night. I questioned if it was sex that he really wanted all along. After trying to convince me of his good intentions, Sam left the house at my request and returned to Bo's place. I went to bed crying.

Two nights later, thanks to Sandy, I was at a get-together surrounded by my closest friends and mentors. It was the exact kind of evening I needed to get my mind off the regret.

With a bag full of her Brazilian nail polish products, Chantel offered top-notch manicures to all the ladies as we sat in a circle and talked about my complicated situation. Each of them showered me in their unique ways with love, uplifting words, and prayer. I felt truly supported.

I expressed that I didn't think Sam deserved to have sex or intimacy, let alone have a second chance at marriage with me. I wanted him to experience the pain of rejection like I had. Instead of gaining up on Sam with me, they encouraged me, reminding me that he was still my husband and that I should see it as a gift that we could comfort each other in such a way. They shared in my sadness and anger but refused to say anything demeaning or judgemental about Sam. They "hated his sin" with me, but they wouldn't hate him, "the sinner."

My friend Andrea looked into my eyes, gently bringing her closed fist into the palm of her hand, and sternly said, "Nia, if you want to forgive Sam, and I think you do, you have to stop thinking about punishing him and begin to think about what it would look like to actually forgive him." At first, her words stung, but as the night Godly wisdom continued, I came around to seeing the truth in their advice.

Their compassion enabled me to think more clearly about my situation. Sam hadn't pressured me at all into having sex with him. We had sex because I allowed it to happen. I needed the intimacy as much as he did.

"There's nothing shameful about wanting that from your husband, Nia," one of the girls said.

As I'd eventually admit to my girls, the entire night I shared with Sam was beautiful and noticeably sweeter than the last intimate moment we shared in Seattle or any other recent time I could recall before it.

Upon arriving home late that night, I sat in the car, trying to decide how I would greet Sam and allow the rest of our night to go. *Should I tell him to pour us another glass of wine,* I thought. Knowing I would return late that night, I agreed that he would stay overnight but sleep in the guest bedroom. I wondered, *what if I told him he could sleep with me tonight?*

When I walked into our impeccably clean home, as was the new normal for me, I quietly made my way to the playroom, automatically thinking I'd catch Sam in the act of betraying me. Instead, I found him lying on the family room floor, seemingly on the verge of falling asleep.

My eyes scanned the room as if to acknowledge his work, but in truth, I was silently praying for the strength to say something kind to him, not necessarily for his sake, but for mine.

Let your words guide your thoughts, I told myself, recalling Andrea's last words to me after saying goodnight.

"The house looks nice," I said, immediately proud of myself. "How'd it go?"

He slowly sat up, sighing as if in pain. "Just a normal day," he responded, looking down at the floor as he fidgeted with a Lego block. "The kids were cute. We had fun."

"What's wrong?" I asked, trying to care. "Tired?"

He took a deep breath and dropped his face into his hands, answering my question without saying a word. He had another confession. "Just tell me," I said.

Behind his hands, he muffled, "I met up with Amy once." He removed his hands and looked up at me. "It was one time. We met in a theater parking lot for about 15 minutes and just talked outside of our cars and caught up."

I was instantly fuming.

Sam and I had long ago agreed that this person was completely off-limits due to the nature of his past "friendship" with her in high school. I thought for sure that Amy was completely in our past and long forgotten. I couldn't have walked into more disappointing news.

"Are you *freakin'* kidding me?" I said, my face feeling flushed. Then, no longer concerned about treating him respectably, I called him a few choice words.

"I'm so sorry that I keep doing this to you," he said. "You don't deserve this."

"Well, nah crap, I don't!" I screamed. "When was this!?" I demanded.

"I think it was during my last semester of nursing school."

I stood silently in the playroom doorway, contemplating my next words. "Did you kiss her?" I asked.

"No!" he exclaimed. "Nothing inappropriate happened."

I clapped my hands to mockingly congratulate him. "I don't believe a word you say anymore!" I screamed as I stormed out of the house and returned to my car.

With my hands shaking, I called Sandy. "Can I stay with you tonight?" I asked. "I have to get out of here. He told me another one."

Forgiving Sam for his stupid, boyish sexual fantasies was easier for me to deal with than the emotional affairs and sneaky rendezvous with old crushes. I spent years feeling like I only had a partial version of the real Sam and now the revelation that it was because he had been giving it away to other women enraged me much worse than his physical unfaithfulness.

When I arrived at Sandy's house, I spent several hours unloading my emotions on her. The bond between Sandy and me was unbreakable; we had weathered countless storms together. As we've matured and become more Christ-like, we've gotten better at supporting each other, pointing to the truth instead of giving in to gossip and drama. But back in high school, she was my war buddy in the heat of the moment, and that's where we went back to that night.

We devised pretend plans on what we'd do if we ever saw one of the girls from Sam's past out in public.

"Home-wrecker on aisle 5!" Sandy joked. Fueled by heartache and confusion, our imaginations came up with some very dark scenarios, even for our past selves.

By the time I fell asleep in Sandy's guest bedroom, I was again certain that I was no longer willing to continue suffering for Sam's past self-centered decisions. Even if he was a changed person, there was just no way I could go on with all this new information and look at him as any more than the man who chose other women over me time and time again.

"I'm divorcing him, Sandy," I said.

30
Sex Ed

*My people have committed two sins: They have forsaken me,
the spring of living water, and have dug their own cisterns,
broken cisterns that cannot hold water.*
Jeremiah 2:13

(Sam)

THE ONLY SEX education I received from my parents came from my mother when I was 15 years old. "You know, Sam," she began nervously, "that's not what sex is really like." She had just found out I looked at pornography on our family computer.

Mortified, I chuckled and replied, "Okay, thanks, Mom," and retreated to my bedroom, never to revisit our conversation.

Initially, I brushed off her wisdom as a misconception, believing that just because she and Dad hadn't had a fulfilling sex life didn't mean sex couldn't be as exciting as it appeared in the movies. But with time, I'd come to regret not hearing more of what Mom had to say.

My emotional reliance on Nia was already at unhealthy levels, but after six months of dating, when we took each other's virginity, my emotional dependence deepened even further. On the surface, this growing attachment to her was exhilarating. Still, beneath the surface, it was a tumor squeezing out not only things I enjoyed, like creating music with my friends, but, more importantly, God's presence from my life. Her touch seemed to be the best remedy to my anxiety and sense of not belonging in the world.

Once we married, after five years of dating, the guilt and shame that once accompanied our sexual encounters were replaced by a strong sense of entitlement and freedom, adding an ecstasy to our relationship that was Hollywood-like. Occasionally, I'd have a twinge of pity for my mother, realizing, based on her mysterious comment to me as a teenager, that she might never have experienced the kind of physical intimacy that Nia and I shared.

My need for Nia's adulation outside and inside the bedroom ran so deep that I began having recurring nightmares about her purposefully dismissing me. Those dreams, it would turn out, were foreboding: deep-seated fears about the inevitable day when my dependence on Nia would no longer hold.

At age 15, when I needed guidance beyond a single obscure statement to help me distinguish between cinematic fantasy and the realities of romantic love, my father was nowhere to be seen. However, the movie collection he left behind was. I found myself captivated by romance films, one of which was *Moulin Rouge,* a musical.

"There was a boy. A very strange, enchanted boy..." the movie began in song. *Wow, that sounds like me*, I thought. It continued, "The greatest thing you'll ever learn is just to love and be loved in return." *I couldn't agree more.* Once the movie finished, I rewinded it and watched it again. Within a month, I knew all the words to all the songs.

I idolized the main character, Christian, the penniless writer, as if he were an older version of myself. His "ridiculous obsession with love" resonated with me like nothing before it. I expected Nia and my relationship to be like the all-consuming romance of this musical, and at first, it was. However, it wasn't long into our marriage before reality set in.

Particularly after the birth of our first child, after "settling down," the well from which I drew my water began producing a less quenchable variety. The deeper elements of that enchanted boy's relationship in *Moulin Rouge* were never displayed on screen; however, it seemed I was beginning to experience them, picking up where the movie left off.

The musical shared plenty about infatuation, but despite the final line, "The greatest thing you'll ever learn is just to love and be loved in return," it left the viewer with the question, "But how?" That was when I began to consider that there might have been truth in my mother's sexual wisdom of old.

Marriage and fatherhood forced me to look into the mirror at all my flaws. I hated what I saw and felt the hurdles before me were far too big to overcome. As if I weren't daunted enough, having recently graduated from nursing school, I quickly realized I had chosen the wrong profession. The downward spiral into depression began.

Unwilling, maybe even incapable, of adapting to reality, I fantasized once again about recreating scenes from my favorite movies or perhaps even the best moments of Nia's and my past relationship. Instead of proactively seeking counsel, I defaulted to what I knew best: chasing women. However, as a married Christian man who still truly loved his wife and family, it didn't go as expected.

The women who responded to my extramarital advances provided me with nothing near the satisfaction that I thought was achievable in my head. Never once did they quench my thirst like Nia was once able to. The initial chase may have been exciting, but once over, I was met with women as selfish as I was, with just as much baggage, if not more than what I had to bring to the table of an affair.

There were reasons these women were giving a married man their attention: they had issues like me and unrealistic fantasies of their own. Both parties were only interested in taking what they could from the other, making for some profoundly unsatisfying encounters.

I soon realized that Nia had, and still was, offering me as much as any woman humanly could. The fantasies in my head were just that: fantasies. I was being lied to, and my fanciful imagination perpetuated them. My heart wasn't craving to return to childish desires and simple ways; it was desiring something superior to human flesh. However, the deceptions ran too deep.

After several failed attempts at romance, the lies of pornography jumped in the driver's seat. I began to assume it was mere sex with random women who I knew nothing about that would bring excitement back into my life. So, I tried visiting massage parlors.

Seconds into starting intercourse for the first time with a prostitute at one of these massage parlors, the woman directing me to do so, I was rendered physically incapable of continuing. Never before had a single moment made me feel as lowly as a rodent as that night. I left the parlor with the bitter taste of rotten fruit in my mouth, having forever defiled mine and Nia's marriage bed, all for an attempt at a fleeting thrill that turned out to steal from me rather than give. Unfortunately, it didn't stop me from going back and giving it another chance.

Months later, I handed a woman ten $20 bills on my fourth visit to a sex worker establishment. Within minutes of being alone in the room with her, once again trying to force a lie into existence, I threw my hands up and said I couldn't go on. She returned my money after I apologized, and then I walked out into a dark alleyway, more frustrated and hopeless about life than ever.

Nothing satisfies, I confessed. As a Christian, I knew it was God I was after, but He didn't seem as exciting or as easy to approach as women and sex were.

I drove home, my heart not only feeling sick for the family I betrayed but also feeling sick for the woman whose soul I clearly cared less about than my sexual exploration. It would be the last time I'd ever attempt to exchange money for sex.

I finally grasped what my mom meant by, "That's not what sex is really like." I didn't ask her questions, and now I was at risk of losing everything. As I once heard, "Sex outside of true love thrills, but it kills. It fascinates, but then it annihilates."

"So what *is* sex really like, Mom?" I wish I had asked.

I think she would have responded, "Real sex is kept within marriage. It is unselfish at its core, seeking the other person's pleasure over yourself. It is more blessed *and* pleasurable to give than to receive in real sex. It's a holy physical oneness that is fulfilled only after whole life oneness."

Now that I was finally emotionally and spiritually naked with Nia, becoming physically naked with her took on a new level of meaning. Nia may have regretted the night we made love before she made her final decision to stay married to me, but it was the best sex we had ever had.

31
Final Indecision

For I know the plans I have for you," says the Lord.
"They are plans for good and not for disaster,
to give you a future and a hope.
Jeremiah 29:11

(Nia)

IT WAS A muggy summer morning. I stepped onto our front porch with my Bible and a steaming cup of coffee. I had an hour to myself after Sam left to take Symphony to school. He spent the previous night at Pastor Bo's place but had arrived before dawn that morning to help with morning routines.

We had made a pact never to mention the "D word" in our marriage, but there I was, doing the unimaginable and seriously considering it. Since I was a young girl, I desperately hoped divorce would never be a part of my life story, but amid the nightmare of Sam's infidelity, it didn't seem like such a bad option after all.

Everyone saw Sam's remorse, so I understood their hopes even if they didn't say it out loud: They wanted me to give Sam another chance. Not to mention, we had two children caught in the middle. However, more than anyone else, I cared what God's opinion was.

Given the history of my grandparents' rocky marriage and other family relationships, biblical divorce was a topic I had researched off and on over the years. It had become an ongoing curious topic for me. Questions like, "Was their divorce justified?" and "Were both, or just one party, allowed to remarry?" and "Did someone have to die first?" were some of the questions that caught my interest.

I knew enough to know that divorce was allowed in cases of infidelity, but I needed to remind myself of the specifics. So, with my highlighter in hand, I opened the Bible and started fervently searching it, expecting God Himself to look me straight in the eyes and say, "Nia, divorce Sam."

I highlighted Matthew 5:32, which says, "But I say that a man who divorces his wife unless she has been unfaithful, causes her to commit adultery..." What stood out to me for the first time was that although Jesus seemed to be saying that the consequences of divorce are *different* when adultery is involved, He wasn't necessarily permitting divorce. This was a confusing eye-opener for me and caused a pile-up of more questions.

Suppose I divorce Sam and eventually remarry, I wondered, *even if I was justified in doing so in God's eyes, will I be putting Sam in a position to commit adultery again if he remarries?* Also, I wondered if the verse implies that anyone who marries a divorced person is also committing adultery. *Will I be perpetuating sin if I choose to divorce Sam?*

The only thing that seemed somewhat clear to me was that if Sam and I both married someone else after divorcing—which was likely—at least one person involved would be in a marriage that dishonored God. At least, that's how I understood it.

I opened my Bible to a few other familiar verses on divorce. First Corinthians says, "A wife must not separate from her husband." I couldn't find any exceptions given there. Then I read in Malachi, "I hate divorce, says the Lord..." *Wow. Definitely no exceptions there, either.*

But it was Matthew 19:6, which says, "What God has joined together, let no one separate," that caused me to close my Bible in frustration.

I leaned back in our porch swing, and before I could even start praying, another question came up. *Does the option of divorce still apply if my husband is truly sorry and is living for the Lord?* From what Sam had shown me thus far, he was committed to doing whatever it took to repair our marriage. I stopped asking questions and started praying.

God, please, I began, looking up at the big oak tree in our front yard, *make it clear to me. Is it wrong to divorce Sam? Should I? I want to make the best decision, but I don't think I could ever trust him again. Please give me more guidance. I may hate Sam, but I love you.*

As Sam pulled into the driveway, I grabbed my Bible and hurried back to my bedroom, closing the door and locking it behind me. It was a huge contrast to when, less than a month ago, I ran towards him when he arrived home, excited to jump into his arms.

I showered, got ready for a birthday celebration with friends, and accepted that even if God was trying to give me His answer, which I felt he wasn't, I was not ready to receive it.

Upon arriving home late that night, I sat with Sandy in her car in my driveway, still unsure about my next move. "Do I stay or do I go?" I blurted out, staring into the dark sky out my window.

I shared with Sandy the whirlwind of thoughts that had been taking over my mind for the past several days. "I wish God would just write *yes* or *no* in the stars for me," I added. Indecisiveness was already a trait I was notorious for, and this decision felt like a life-or-death one that could mess up many lives if I got it wrong.

Then, suddenly, a wave of clarity came over me.

I already gave you the answer.

Huh? I wondered.

A loud gasp escaped me as I realized the words were from the Lord, right away knowing what "answer" He was referring to.

I looked at Sandy with my mouth wide open in shock.

"What!? She exclaimed.

A memory from a month earlier raced through my mind as I stared into her eyes.

****

A young woman in our church, whom I deeply cared for, had become pregnant, and I was invited to her baby shower. While I wanted to celebrate this significant moment with her, I didn't think I could see her baby bump and all the baby things while mourning my miscarriage without breaking down in public. My heart was still broken, my womb still heavy with emptiness, and my mind still foggy with grief.

"Come on, let's just go together," a friend texted me the morning of the baby shower. "Maybe it will be good for you."

After Sam encouraged me to take her up on her offer, I released a heavy sigh and replied, "Okay, fine."

Upon arriving at the baby shower, I was met at the door by women I loved and looked up to, most of whom were women in leadership in our church. They immediately showed an incredible amount of sensitivity and kindness to me, fully aware that I was still in the process of grieving.

Their encouraging words and gestures made it easier for me to relax and to be fully present. I was soon surprised by how therapeutic it was to touch and look at all the tiny baby things, including my friend's baby bump. Then, as joy replaced my sadness and I mingled more and more, something unusual started happening.

One by one, different women pulled me aside into private conversations about their marriages. At the drink station, one woman told me about a financial issue in her marriage, wondering what she should do next as a wife. After giving some small advice from my experience, I went to the sink to wash my hands.

While there, another woman began to confide in me about her sex life not being at a healthy place and how badly she wanted things to turn around for her and her husband. I gave her some encouragement and my best advice, and she seemed blessed by what I had to say. We hugged and went our separate ways.

Later, while refilling my plate at the charcuterie bar, I talked with another woman who told me that she had discovered her husband connecting with a woman on Facebook. After offering advice and reminding her of her worth, I sat on the couch, reflecting on my unexpected role of building up other women.

Within minutes of sitting on the couch alone, a woman in her 20s sat beside me and began sharing the ups and downs of her dating life. After our conversation, she stood up, tears in her eyes, and thanked me for taking the time to listen.

I was totally thrown off guard by what was happening. As basically a newlywed among most of these women, I had always been the one seeking their marital wisdom. Yet, there I was, attracting them with their important questions and offering them wisdom that appeared to genuinely uplift them.

Sitting alone on the sofa in Chantel's living room, I began to pray. *Lord, what in the world is happening? I've never been on this side of these conversations before. Who am I that these wise, Godly women would trust me with their private information and value my input?*

As I prayed, the conversations around me became muffled as if a thick glass wall suddenly divided me from everybody else. A hot flash came over my body, and my heart started racing. Then, as if He were sitting right beside me, I heard the Holy Spirit say, "You and Sam will be in marriage ministry."

Up to this point, the Holy Spirit had only clearly spoken to me a few times before, on a much smaller scale, and only while reading the Bible. Minor instances compared to what was happening on that couch.

Wait, what? I asked. *There's no way.*

Ministry refers to focusing on the specific needs of people within the church, while marriage ministry focuses on supporting marriages. A part of me was excited by the news, but I prayed we aren't *equipped or experienced enough for something like that.* Sam and I had a decent marriage, but I was sure we weren't a couple that anybody else would care to emulate. Our communication alone needed tons of work.

The message didn't make much sense to me, but since I was sure it was from the Lord, I did my best not to doubt it. I must have felt similar to how Mary felt when told she had found favor with God. "How can this be?" she asked. The angel responded that nothing was impossible with God. I wanted my response to be like Mary's: "Behold, I am the servant of the Lord; let it be to me according to your word."

When I returned home that night, I sat down in front of Sam, who was stretched out comfortably across our bed. "Okay," I began. "Can I say something crazy?"

"Well, yeah," Sam laughed.

"Today at the baby shower," I said, "I'm pretty positive that the Holy Spirit told me that you and I will be in marriage ministry one day."

"Interesting," Sam slowly said with skepticism in his voice. "Are you sure?" After I assured him that my experience was real, he chuckled and asked, "What could we possibly offer other marriages? I barely know what I'm doing as it is."

His response was disappointing.

Although the idea of helping other marriages seemed exciting to me, I knew Sam had a valid point. We moved on to a different topic, and by morning, I decided I wouldn't mention it again, writing it off as hopeful thinking.

****

God already gave me the answer, I told myself as Sandy stared back at me.

"Tell me!" Sandy exclaimed.

"I really need to go," I told her. I'll call you tomorrow and tell you. I feel really overwhelmed right now." While I was pleasantly surprised by God's clear communication with me, I was equally disappointed by what He said.

I was far from prepared to recommit myself to spending my life with Sam and felt nowhere near ready to forgive him. Was God suggesting that I'd have to climb this seemingly insurmountable mountain before getting to the place of helping other marriages? God gave me the answer to my question, but only half of the answer was what I would have hoped for.

It just doesn't seem possible, God, I prayed. *I can barely handle the idea of Sam thinking another woman is pretty, and you want me to move past him cheating on me multiple times?!*

I continued to doubt what I heard. *If this is really from you, please give me a clearer sign.*

32
Holey Blouse

Whenever someone turns to the Lord, the veil is taken away.
Wherever the Spirit of the Lord is, there is freedom.
Ephesians 4:2-3

(Sam)

NIA DIDN'T HAVE to spell it out for me to know that my crimes were perpetually on her mind or that she feared another betrayal could strike her again at any moment. No matter how valid I thought they were, I became ultra-sensitive to her concerns.

During this time of repair, rebuilding, and healing, my sole purpose was to create and maintain a protective bubble around Nia and our marriage, even if it came at the cost of other valuable relationships in our lives, which it soon would.

Whereas I used to walk on eggshells as I kept my secrets hidden, I was now just as cautious in ensuring Nia knew I had nothing left to hide, being extra careful to avoid doing anything that could be misconstrued as a sign of unfaithfulness.

Simple acts like spraying on cologne, keeping my phone in my pocket, or being alone in a room required careful consideration. Whenever I considered styling my hair or brushing my teeth outside the usual times, I'd assume Nia feared I was getting ready to meet another woman, so instead, I'd throw on a hat and accept having slimy teeth. As another measure of my transparency to Nia, I went so far as to leave the bathroom door open when using it. Initially, this cautious way of living was solely about providing a healthy environment for Nia as she healed, but it quickly evolved into something unexpected.

As I improved at living sacrificially for my wife, my love and devotion to her grew as well. I already loved Nia immensely, but as I put off my old self, pushing aside selfish tendencies for the sake of her security, she became all the more precious to me. I wasn't sure what was happening, but I loved loving her more and more.

In addition to this surprising benefit, the more I served Nia, the more I felt *worthy* of serving her, something the guilt I had harbored for most of our marriage likely prevented me from experiencing in the past. My secrets had caused more damage to my heart than I realized. They kept me from experiencing the beauty that love offers to the spouse giving it.

While doing a load of laundry, Nia resting in the next room, I called out, "This dryer doesn't have a dial?"

"The flat side of the metal thing needs to face the opposite direction of what you want to select," Nia explained. "Use the pliers on the shelf. Also, the door sometimes pops open, so you have to lean something against it."

I later noticed rust spots inside the washer, and it didn't seem to wring out the clothes all the way. Nia had never mentioned these issues, but I felt regretful that she had been managing with such outdated appliances for so long. Luckily, we were in a financial position for me to change that.

Entering the room where Nia sat, I apologized. "I'm sorry you've had to use that old washer and dryer," I said while sliding on my flip-flops. "I'm going to go buy you a new set."

"Are you serious?" Nia said, trying to hold back a smile.

"Absolutely!" I exclaimed.

"Wow," she said. "Cool."

As usual, I wasn't about to leave the house alone so abruptly, aware it might raise obvious suspicions for Nia. Before confessing everything to Nia, I had struggled to bond with Abram on account of his colic, seldom making an effort. Perhaps it had been my secrets, I acknowledged, that had actually been the barrier to my relationship with him, and I truly was only as patient as I was honest. Regardless, I gained a new appreciation for my children and felt a renewed capacity to love them better.

I changed Abram, dressed him, and loaded him in the car for a trip to Home Depot. Taking this kind of initiative in my home marked a significant milestone. What started as an attempt to free me from the snare of my secrets and then to provide a safe space for my wife's healing turned into me becoming a better husband, father, and leader all around. I was forced to look in the mirror again, but this time, God also stared back at me, making my inadequacies appear insignificant.

I was finally embracing my role as an inexperienced adult, moving beyond the fear of failing or appearing foolish, willing to learn as I went. I prayed that the days when I felt hopeless of becoming a healthy, functioning man were long behind me. I was no longer a slave to fear.

Would Nia believe my efforts were merely superficial attempts to momentarily pacify her? I was determined not to allow those kinds of defeating thoughts to interfere with my actions. Besides, first and foremost, I was serving the Lord. Also, I needed to know for myself that my attempts at earning her trust were sincere.

Nia watched with reserved excitement as I set up her new washer and dryer, standing by with her arms crossed over her chest, a restrained smile on her face. Nia wouldn't be easily tricked again, nor would I allow it if it was within my power to prevent it. Buying some shiny new appliances wasn't suddenly going to change our situation, nor did I expect it to, but still, I wasn't going to stop acting on my urges to treat her the best I knew how. If the idea was good, I acted on it.

After pushing the appliances into place, I emptied our hamper into the washer and started a cycle. As the remarkably quiet load finished, I observed that many of Nia's clothes, particularly her undergarments, appeared old and worn.

"Nia," I stated, holding up a blouse with an obvious hole in it, "This is unacceptable. You need to go out right now and buy yourself some new clothes." I didn't have to ask her twice. The next morning, she went out shopping for a new wardrobe with her friends.

While she was gone, my friend Erick and I cleaned up the flower beds in front of our house, planting fresh flowers and shrubs. When we were done, the kids and I decorated the driveway with sidewalk chalk, leaving messages of appreciation for Nia. After putting the kids to bed, I cleaned the house, intent on making everything sparkle on her return.

With shopping bags draped over her shoulders, Nia approached the front, radiating a happiness and gratitude I hadn't seen in her since the day before my confessions to her two weeks prior. Her gaze fell upon her new flower bed. "It's beautiful," she said.

As she entered the house that smelled brand new, she turned to me with misty eyes and said something that overwhelmed me with emotion.

"You've been so sweet to me," she said after dropping her bags, covering her face with her hands.

I didn't deserve to hear those words; the things I was doing should have been done long ago, but they immediately brought me to tears. I walked over and wrapped her up as she sobbed into my shoulder. I reassured her of my undying love for her and reminded her that I was no longer the man I had described in my confessions.

"I know you may think I'm doing this stuff just to win you back," I said, "but I hope time will show how much I truly love you." I wouldn't need much time at all.

An opportunity to demonstrate my physical and emotional faithfulness to her was on the horizon.

33
Shiny Boxes

*As the bridegroom rejoices over the bride,
so shall your God rejoice over you.
Isaiah 62:5*

(Nia)

DRIVING TO BEBO'S house one evening, I passed Haskell Lane, the road that led to one of the spots where Sam had met with one of the women from his confessions. The mere thought, let alone the sight of the road, enraged me.

"I was probably washing his clothes when he met her there," I said aloud, gritting my teeth.

Although my heart was beginning to soften towards Sam, this road sent me back to square one. I felt powerless to images flooding my mind of him and this woman taking the drive together, greeting each other, holding hands, and then saying their goodbyes.

These types of triggers were far from exclusive to this road. They seeped into nearly all aspects of my life: places, songs, clothes, food, friends, family, and even Sam's face. Each of them would send me spiraling into a unique sense of rejection without a moment's notice.

The pain seemed so deeply rooted that when I prayed for it to leave, I doubted God could uproot it. *Could you at least give me something else to think about instead?* I'd beg, doubting that that much was even possible. Could a new, tolerable memory replace a memory that caused me such deep inner turmoil?

A few days later, driving with my kids in the backseat, headed toward Haskell Lane and dreading every second, I screamed inside, *I can't take it anymore! Replace these memories, God.* Then, as the road came into view, it felt as though heaven opened up and shone a light right into my car. Lyrics on the radio sang out in perfect timing: "You are His bride." It was a shocking moment and felt too beautiful to be a coincidence.

"I am *his* bride," I reminded myself out loud as the song continued. "I belong to *Jesus* and not to anything or *anyone* else."

During that moment of clarity, a beautiful memory I hadn't revisited in many years was handed to me like a tangible gift straight from Jesus, a shiny box, as I would come to call them.

A few weeks after our son was born, we had a family photoshoot done at a local park. The park was nestled at the end of an old neighborhood cul-de-sac. An open golden field stretched out for a mile behind it. This was the place where we posed as a family of four for the first time. I remembered that during that photoshoot, I had been in the middle of postpartum depression, and for the first time in months, God granted me an overflowing sense of gratitude and hope, offering me a brief respite from my dark thoughts. The location of that special photoshoot had taken place right off none other than Haskell Lane.

Just like that, God gave me something hopeful and beautiful to replace my tortuous thoughts: A shiny box with a precious memory inside. I drove past the road with a moist smile on my face.

Thank you, Lord. You're so gracious.

After that day, I began eagerly looking for redemptive moments to replace other triggers in my life. These shiny boxes would usually be handed to me while I was wide-eyed, prayerful, and receptive to redemption. But one day, I had a shiny box moment when I least expected it.

After an overnight girls' trip, I was driving through Dallas on my way home with Sandy and Lauren when a billboard caught our attention: "Beautycon Dallas." The last day of the conference was happening right then. Lauren Googled the event, got three free tickets, and rerouted us to the venue.

On our way, we decided that coffee was in order since we were extending our evening, so I mapped the closest Starbucks. Once we arrived, we learned the coffee shop was attached to a large fancy hotel. We wandered around and took selfies together before ordering our drinks.

Like slow-motion cogs shown in movies sometimes, I looked up at the blue glass-covered building and was reminded that Sam had confessed to hanging out with a woman in the lobby of a hotel in Dallas. I whirled around to see the hotel's name on a large sign, and it hit me: this was that very hotel.

I nervously walked backward into my girlfriend's arms and, with hands over my mouth, said, "This is a moment, you guys. God is doing something here."

I started crying as I explained that Sam had been there with another woman, causing my girlfriends to cry with me. I explained that God was replacing that horrible memory right then with the fun memories I was making with them at that moment. Their beautiful faces were the new memory replacing the old one. I couldn't believe it. We didn't even plan to be there; it was so last minute, and there God was, giving me another shiny box out of nowhere.

From then on, that hotel would be remembered as the place where I spontaneously got coffee and wandered around with my girlfriends and not as the place where my husband chose another woman over me.

Thank you, God, for your healing power in my life.

I looked up to see a faint grin on Lauren's face as she glanced up from her phone. With almost an arrogant tone, she met my eyes and said, "You'll never guess where Beautycon is."

"Where?!" I asked excitedly as I dried my eyes.

"Right inside this building!" she screamed.

"No way!" Sandy and I screamed back.

We returned to the lobby, passed through another set of double doors, and found ourselves in awe as we walked deeper into the excitement of Beautycon Dallas.

Over the next several hours, we were pampered to the nines. We had makeovers, our hair done, photo shoots with cute backdrops, and even met a real celebrity. The outward transformation of our appearances resembled the makeover God was giving to my heart that night.

I would have been satisfied with the simple memory of having coffee with my friends, but He took it a step further, as He always does, and gave me an entire evening of unmatched girly fun with my best friends. God was wooing me.

The next day, Sam called me, delivering news that threatened to erase all the hope that had been restored to me the previous day. I had believed that his slip-ups and struggles were in his past; in his call, however, I learned they were very much a part of his present and future. When we hung up, I couldn't help but wonder if the news was

the final confirmation I had been seeking.
   Is divorcing Sam the best path forward for me?

34

Temptation Test

*To those who lack good judgment, she says,
"Stolen water is refreshing; food eaten in secret tastes the best!"
But little do they know that the dead are there.
Proverbs 9:16-18*

(Sam)

NIA AND I pulled up to the curb of the home where our church community group would be meeting, each in our own car. As the evening of fellowship with our friends drew to a close and it was time to leave, my car refused to start.

Nia and I headed home together, leaving my car parked on the curb.

The following day, after being dropped off by Nia, I sat in my disabled car, waiting for the scheduled tow truck to arrive.

I texted Heath, "I should be at the mechanic in 45 minutes." We had planned to resume our discussion from the previous week and dive into another chapter of *Crazy Love* by Francis Chan.

Upon looking up from my phone, I spotted the homeowner, Lisa, a woman in her late thirties who had hosted our community group the night before, emerge from her home dressed in her workout attire. She began walking towards my vehicle through her freshly cut lawn.

"Hey, Sam," she said as she drew closer. "What the heck are you doing sitting out here?"

I responded, "My car wouldn't start last night. Pretty sure it's my starter. I'm just waiting for the tow truck to get here."

"Well come inside and wait," she said.

"Umm," I stammered.

"Come on," she insisted, gesturing towards her house as she began to walk towards it, "It's too hot out here. Seriously, come inside."

My heart pounded. I glanced down her driveway and noticed her husband's car wasn't there. I felt the gravitational pull of my old ways. *It could be fun,* they whispered. Before they could say another word, I shook it off. "Oh, no, thank you," I said.

"Are you sure?" Lisa asked as she made her way back to my car.

"Yeah, I'm just going to wait in my car and edit some photos," I said.

She eyeballed my camera in the passenger seat and asked me about the lenses I preferred. We briefly discussed photography equipment, after which she said, "I used to do portrait photography, too, you know?"

"Oh, that's cool," I said, hoping not to extend our private conversation.

"Come inside!" she demanded. "I'll show you my work and get you some water."

I took a deep breath as my heart began to race again. I didn't feel any romantic or physical attraction toward this woman, and I didn't sense she had any toward me. However, I knew that situations like these had the potential to cause those types of feelings to develop.

Fully aware of my old habit of allowing women to become emotional homes for me, that I was still vulnerable, I knew long before that moment that I would need more than mere willpower to resist falling back into them. Hence, boundaries: avoiding situations long before my emotions would be tested.

As I gazed through my windshield, the invitation hanging in the air between us, all I could think was, *how do I decline her offer without sounding accusatory?* I had to see this woman again on Sunday morning.

One of the lines I highlighted in the book *Crazy Love* that day was, "God doesn't call us to be comfortable. He calls us to trust Him so completely that we are unafraid to put ourselves in situations where we will be in trouble if He doesn't come through." While it likely wasn't what Francis Chan had in mind, I realized that sharing the truth of my situation with Lisa would place me in a very uncomfortable position. Yet, it would force me to trust God.

"I really can't," I began. "It's just not appropriate since our spouses aren't here."

"It's not like that, you ding dong," she said.

I took another deep breath. "Yeah, I know," I murmured, "but Nia and I are actually in the middle of fighting for our marriage right now…" *Am I really telling her this?* "…after I recently confessed to her that I was unfaithful to her several years back." *I guess so.*

"Oh," she said, dumbfounded and clearly embarrassed. "Okay?"

"Going into your house would set us back no matter what the intentions are," I added. "It's just not wise."

An awkward silence ensued.

"That's fine," she said enthusiastically, "I'll just go get the photos."

As she turned and walked away, the built-up cringe inside me made me sink deep into my seat. "Hurry up, you dumb tow truck," I whimpered.

Minutes later, she walked out of her house with a stack of bulky picture frames, apparently having taken them off her walls. *This can't be real life,* I thought.

I pretended to be interested in the photos as she awkwardly held each one up.

"Those are good," I remarked, trying not to laugh out of utter embarrassment.

"Thanks," she said as she fumbled with the picture frames. "Well, it was good seeing ya."

"Yeah, you too," I said, excited that the mortifying moment was ending. "I'll see ya later."

After my nerves settled and I thanked God that it was over, I called Nia and told her everything that had unfolded.

"I'm not mad at you," Nia assured me, "I'm just angry that there was even an option for you to go inside with her."

"Yeah, I understand," I said.

"I bet you wanted to go inside with her, didn't you?" Nia asked.

"I didn't even consider it," I said. "I knew I wasn't going to cross that boundary, and that's all I was focused on."

Nia sighed. "I haven't even finished processing your old confessions, and new ones are already popping up. I guess this is my new life. I gotta go." Nia hung up without saying goodbye.

Despite Nia's disappointment, I knew this was a win for us. I got to show her firsthand that I was putting my money where my mouth was.

Minutes later, the tow truck arrived. Heath picked me up from the mechanic, and we headed to a Starbucks together.

I felt accomplished, closer to God, one step closer to earning Nia's trust, and excited about continuing *Crazy Love*.

35
Pestilence

Though a thousand fall at your side,
though ten thousand are dying around you,
these evils will not touch you.
Psalms 91:7

(Nia)

"DID YOU SEE anyone you know today?" I asked.
Sam answered no.
"Have any girls reached out to you?" I asked.
Sam answered no.
"I bet you *want* me to divorce you, don't you?" I asked.
Sam answered no.
"You're still thinking about Tracy, aren't you?" I asked.
Sam answered no.
I bombarded Sam with questions, doubting his loyalty and motivation at the snap of a finger. I never knew when I'd erupt in bitterness, but when I did, Sam was the first to know.
When I believed his efforts were genuine, I'd get angry that I was getting this new Sam *after* he cheated on me and then convince myself that he didn't deserve the fruit of being the better man he claimed to be.

I held back from showing him appreciation, making sure he knew I felt he was doing the bare minimum after what he did to me. With the immense pressure my suspicions placed on Sam, I expected him to give up at any moment. However, as days progressed into weeks, his devotion to our marriage continued without losing intensity.

Sam had made promises I thought he could never keep, and if he did, I figured they'd be inconsistent or short-lived at best. He slowly proved me wrong. I'd be lying if I said his efforts didn't play a significant part in softening my heart, but I give God credit for helping me begin seeing Sam through the lens through which He saw him.

Who was I to continue to hold Sam's sins against him if God had done the complete opposite with his sins? Sam was clearly repentant; therefore, as the Bible says, God is faithful and just and will forgive him. I was obviously expected to do the same.

The recognition of Sam's relentless efforts to remove the wedge he had driven between us hit me hard. The Holy Spirit, helping me discern between bitterness and pain, convicted me of forming my own wedge in our marriage, which only worsened our divide.

I started thinking about all the ways Sam had changed. He filled the house with worship music, prayed openly for me and the kids, read the Bible to us nightly, and ensured we never missed church or community group. He was enthusiastic about his new life of living in truth; his candid honesty and his Bible, which was constantly nearby and open, were the biggest signs of that.

Sam became transparent with me in ways he had never been before. I had grown used to vague and surface-level answers to my questions, and finally, I was getting detailed, vulnerable, Godly, and heartfelt responses from him.

Were these strong, convicting emotions the final sign I had asked for from the Lord? Was he telling me to stop considering divorce and now work on forgiveness and healing?

That night, before Sam headed to our guest bedroom, I gave him a small kiss to encourage him. "Thank you for staying patient with me," I said.

"As long as it takes," he replied.

I then went to our bedroom alone and opened up my Bible.

As I read Psalm 91 and reached verse seven, an adrenaline surge rushed through me as I made connections and received insights from the Lord in a beautifully unexpected way. Psalm 91:5-7 says,

You will not fear the terror of night, nor the arrow that

flies by day, nor the pestilence that stalks in the darkness, nor the plague that destroys at midday. A thousand may fall at your side, ten thousand at your right hand, but it will not come near you.

While reading, my mind substituted the word "pestilence" with the word "divorce." This prompted me to do a quick search for divorce statistics in America.

According to the CDC, there were 2,221,579 marriages in 2015. In that same year, there were almost a million divorces, about 30% of them likely due to infidelity.

Tens of thousands were literally falling around me. I began to see divorce as a modern-day pestilence spreading like a highly contagious virus.

The effects of divorce reach into generations—Sam and I both are living examples of it— negatively affecting countless children, making this pestilence, in my view, more severe than any other. If I wanted God to protect my family from disease, which I often did, why wasn't I actively praying against the home-wrecking disease of divorce?

I reread the verses, and this time, I felt the Holy Spirit telling me, *Hey Nia, stop worrying. This disease isn't going to touch you.* A wave of freedom hit me. It was like I could finally take a deep breath again. Fear and worry melted away as I sat in God's presence.

My home was safe from divorce. His blood was on our doorpost. I fell asleep thanking God for being my refuge and showing me the way out of my bitterness and unwillingness to forgive Sam.

The next day, in high spirits, before anyone else woke up, I headed to the gym to clear my mind and think over, one last time, whether staying with Sam was truly what God wanted for me.

As I jogged on the treadmill, an unusual wave of exhaustion and nausea came over me, and I was suddenly flooded with worry all over again. "There's no way," I mumbled to myself, trying not to break down in tears as I turned off the treadmill.

I had experienced the same symptoms several times before, and each time, it was the beginning of a highly complex journey for my health, full of unknowns, several doctor visits, and usually ending in major surgery.

Can this really be happening right now? I wondered, trying not to panic.

Nervous about my future, I grabbed my belongings, jumped into my car, and drove to the nearest drugstore. There was only one way to know for sure if my life truly was on the verge of changing dramatically in a whole other way.

Without informing anyone, I purchased the test and took it home. I locked myself in the bathroom and followed the instructions. After getting the results several minutes later, I loudly gasped, "Oh my gosh," throwing my hands over my mouth.

The timing swirled in my mind like a tornado. It seemed too crazy to be true. I fought back tears as I asked God what He was doing. Almost immediately, I felt like I received His reply: *Trust me.*

Right then, it was as if God forced the option of divorce right out of my hands and threw it. I finally surrendered it to Him. The option of divorce left me once and for all.

Okay, God, I prayed. *I'm sorry for resisting your obvious will for me, but now what?*

After putting the kids to bed that evening, I finally worked up the nerve to tell Sam the news. I paused mid-stride in the living room's entryway, looked at Sam doing the dishes, and said, "You're not going to believe this."

"You're pregnant?!" he exclaimed with an exaggerated smile.

"What!?" I asked, "How the heck did you know?!"

"No way!?" he said.

I laughed through misty eyes. "I really am.

He jumped up and threw his arms around me, lifting me off the floor. "This is amazing! Praise God!" he screamed.

"I almost thought you tested my urine again," I laughed.

As he set me back down, tears welling in both our eyes, he asked, "How can this be? We only did it one time."

I was just as shocked. We hadn't used protection for almost a year before Sam finally got his positive result from my toilet water, and already, after a single time of making love over the period of a month, two blue lines stared back at me.

After several minutes of being amazed together, I decided it was the perfect time to share with him everything the Lord had been revealing to me. I reminded him of the baby shower moment, where I felt the Lord had told me he and I would be in marriage ministry one day. I then explained the significance of this positive pregnancy test to me and how both instances were clear indicators from God of the eventual redemption of our marriage. Then I said what I once thought would never come out of my mouth.

"The D-word is off the table."

Sam lifted me off the floor again, and our tears flowed even harder.

"Praise God again!" He said through joyful laughter.

I decided to stay with Sam and even began openly appreciating who he had become, at the same time deciding not to allow bitterness to have a place in my heart. The dynamics in our home shifted significantly, especially after I invited him back into our bedroom. His efforts to regain my trust, his transparent communication with me, and his desire for God did not die down. However, the initial excitement of embarking on the path of forgiveness and renewal faded quickly for me.

Sam's confessions continued to gnaw at me, sparking an intense internal battle between the enemy's lies and God's truth. The journey of forgiveness and complete reconciliation turned out to be a completely different beast than the grieving and acceptance phase, more challenging and prolonged than I could have predicted.

In the meantime, Sam and I continued our YouTube journey, reaching new highs and being presented with more once-in-a-lifetime opportunities. However, it wasn't long before we started hitting new lows. Depression struck our home once again, but in a new way, leaving us vulnerable to old ways.

PART 6
Eden Reclaimed
The final confession

36
Wake-Up Crash

*For we are his workmanship, created in Christ Jesus
for good works, which God prepared beforehand,
that we should walk in them.*
Ephesians 2:10

(Nia)

THE BLARING HISPANIC music drowned out everyone's conversations except those I had with myself in my head. The familiar taste of jealousy was in my mouth.

Sam just cracked a joke. Will he glance at Amy to see if she's laughing at him?

Sam and I were at Carmona's, a Tex-Mex restaurant, having a celebratory dinner with our church youth group. We were both still in high school. I was a sophomore; he was a senior. We sat across from each other in the center of a long table, picking at the chips and salsa after having finished our meals, trying to hear our youth leader tell stories at the end of the table.

Sitting two seats down from Sam was Amy, a former "friend" of his and the person whose family he lived with at the time.

Two months into my relationship with Sam as his girlfriend, a year before this evening, he had confessed to me over the phone that, contrary to what he previously told me, he and Amy had been more than just friends before we met. I was hurt. Out of respect for me, he agreed to distance himself from Amy as much as he could from then on.

As our server dropped off the bills, she delivered with them the very reason we had chosen Carmona's for dinner: free dessert. Receiving a little white carton of icy rainbow sherbet after a plate of spicy food was what I had been looking forward to all evening.

"Man, that was truly delectable," Sam joked after taking his last bite. "I need more."

Without skipping a beat, Amy said, "Here, have the rest of mine," as she slid her unfinished sherbet over to Sam.

To my shock, Sam picked up the carton. "Oh, thanks," he said.

I put on a smile and clenched my teeth as I watched Sam dig into the sherbet. Amy straightened up in her seat, seemingly proud of appeasing my man, then awkwardly glared in my direction.

"I have to use the restroom," I said.

I stood in front of the restroom mirror and watched myself take several deep breaths, allowing my anger to show through. I wanted to scream. *Why couldn't Sam have been man enough to say no,* I thought.

I exited the restroom and mouthed, "Thank goodness," when I saw our group standing at the cash register, getting ready to leave.

After saying our goodbyes, Sam and I got into my brand-new 2004 Toyota Corolla, a gift from my parents for my 16th birthday just six months prior. I slid into the driver's seat.

While pulling out of the parking lot, Sam asked, "Are you Okay?"

"Everything is great," I began sarcastically, "I mean, I didn't get an extra carton of sherbet from Amy like you did." I paused and looked over at Sam, noticing a defeated expression on his face. "Was it worth it?" I added.

My car became nothing more than a prop to help me convey my anger to Sam as I sped down a dark country road toward Amy's house to drop him off.

"Cutie, I have to live with this girl," he said. "What did you expect me to do after saying I wanted more, and she offered me exactly that?"

"What would you do if I took a half-eaten dessert from my ex-boyfriend and ate it happily right in front of your face?" I screamed.

"She's not my ex-girlfriend, and the circumstances are different," he said.

"I'll tell you exactly what you would've done," I continued. You wouldn't have got back in the car with me!"

"Okay," Sam said, "just slow down. I'm sorry."

Mindlessly driving 60 miles per hour in a 30, I continued, "We agreed to stop talking to people we had a past with, and you might as well have kissed her!"

"Oh, come on!" Sam said, "You have to calm down!"

Our conversation was going in circles; before I knew it, so were we.

The asphalt road I was speeding on suddenly turned into loose gravel. I took my foot off the gas and felt like my car was suddenly hovering above the ground.

"Oh my gosh," Sam and I said in unison.

"Don't hit the brake," Sam instructed as he leaned over and grabbed the steering wheel.

In a split-second decision of wanting to bring the demented car to a stop, I slammed my foot on the brake pedal. "Oh no!" I screamed as my car suddenly started drifting sideways.

The car swung us around, sending us swirling in slow, steady spins as if we were on ice, all while moving down the narrow gravel road at an unchanged speed.

"Oh God, please, no!" I screamed as Sam tried to regain control of the car.

After completing two full circles, we were thrown into a steep, dark ditch. The sound of crunching metal rang through the darkness as my body was pulled into the back of my driver's seat.

Everything was suddenly still.

I looked up to see my headlights lighting up a massive cloud of white dust. I reached for Sam's arm, desperately needing to know if he was still alive, "Are you okay? Are you okay?!" I frantically asked. "I love you! I'm so sorry!" I added.

Sam looked around before responding. "I'm fine," he mumbled.

We glanced at the backseat, met by the sight of a shattered rear window inches from our faces and a tree trunk as wide as the car right up against it. My brand new car was completely smashed in from the back.

After getting our doors open, we walked up the ditch and held each other tightly in the middle of the dark, rocky road. From what we were looking at in the ditch, it was clear that we would have been dead had we hit the tree head-on.

I started crying as Sam expressed his frustrations with my careless driving. "I can't believe you, cutie."

As I repeated my apologies to him through my tears, he continued, "Your jealousy almost killed us, and now your brand new car is gone."

After having the owner of a nearby house call for help, the police arrived. They confirmed what we already knew. It was a miracle that we walked out of the wreck unscathed, let alone alive.

The next day, Sam and I replayed the events and realized how fortunate we were to still have each other. I forgave Sam for crossing a boundary with Amy, and he forgave me for putting our lives in danger. We prayed together and thanked God for His protection over us, acknowledging that God obviously had plans for us that hadn't yet been realized. Then confessed that those plans would probably never be realized if we continued to live in sin.

We agreed that the car accident was God's discipline for our disobedience—His way of guiding us back onto the right path. We repented of our sexual impurity and vowed to wait until marriage to have sex again.

The following Monday morning, in between classes, Sam handed me a letter. It read:

Dear my lady Nia.

I miss you like Forever would miss us if we weren't here together to challenge it. I look forward to seeing you like Tomorrow does our beautiful love, and I love you like Today loves the love we spread throughout it. Last night, I cried because I ever hurt you, particularly the Amy thing. You're the only reason I'm happy, and I thank God He sent me someone stronger than myself. I told Erick yesterday that I didn't think there was anyone more honest than me, but I've come to find out that you're as honest as they come. I'm never going to lose you, Nia. Nothing in my life has been as important to me as you are. I want nothing to harm you in any way, especially by me. I won't let it happen again, mark my words. I know this quitting sex and stuff is going to be hard. I got so depressed thinking about all this at lunch. It was all so special, but at least we know how it's going to be when we get married. I love you so much. We have to do this, Nia. I know it will only help us and give us a better life in the future. When you told me we're going to live such a blessed life, I remember thinking that there's no way that will be so if we continue to do the things we're doing and ignore everything we read in the Bible together (Remember Proverbs 29:1? That'll be our verse). I'm so curious where we'll end up and how things are going to be for us. Actually, I can't wait to find out, no matter what it may be. I can't wait till we're living together, me and the whole world under a single roof. God's knocking at my heart, and He has been for as long as I can remember. I'm going to invite Him in now. I love you so much, and a little bit of pleasure just isn't worth our future together. We've only got one life, so let's make it rock together, and when we get married, we'll express our love for each other in that way, but until then, let's ask God to help us plan ahead and do it wisely. I can't wait to see what happens. Niaway, I can't wait to see you, and I'm so happy that the bell is about to ring in about 3 minutes. Oh boy, oh boy, I miss you. Bye, sweetness.

Love always and forever and a day or two, Sam R.

It was only a matter of weeks before Sam and I succumbed to breaking our vow of remaining sexually pure. Our efforts at self-counseling failed to break the cycle of the seemingly physical addiction we had developed for each other. We needed external help, specifically closer adult supervision, to help steer us out of the destructive loop we found ourselves in.

Despite our continued on-and-off-again disobedience, not without consequences along the way, God, in His grace, would still allow Sam and me to witness one of the huge reasons why He had protected our lives on the terrifying night when I totaled my car.

He had a remarkable plan for us, and despite our failures, He would allow us to live it out.

37
Broke

For when I kept silent, my bones wasted away through my groaning all day long.
Psalm 32:3

(Sam)

"COME BACK SAM and Nia" was the petition's title created on Change.org. The description read, "Sam and Nia have endured so much, and all who sign this petition show sympathy for them." The author had no idea about the struggles we were *actually* enduring, especially Nia.

One and a half months after setting our camera down and taking a break from YouTube, putting all efforts and resources into our marriage, Nia and I returned to making vlogs again. Our comeback vlog was innocently titled *Nia Got a Haircut*.

We resumed our vlogs as if nothing had happened, implying to our audience that we had taken the time off to recover from the public backlash regarding our pregnancy and the Ashley Madison ordeal, carefully sidestepping the truth that we had actually been on the brink of divorce.

I assumed that regaining our viewers' attention after all the public scandal and accusations would be difficult, if not impossible. It seemed

I was wrong, at least at first glance. Our channel exploded, reaching higher numbers than ever. We went on to post some of our most-viewed videos to date, several of which outperformed our previous viral hits combined. Our subscriber count soared from 350,000 to 2.5 million over the following three years, surpassing the billion-view milestone.

I focused on producing daily family vlogs and, on the side, working on larger video projects strictly meant to attract new subscribers and generate more revenue. One such project involved transforming our swimming pool into a colossal smiley emoji, a video that now has 63 million views and has brought in a total of $77,000 from AdSense alone.

Throughout this time of chasing numbers, we kept all aspects of our marriage's healing journey behind closed doors. While keeping this private would be expected, our situation was unique. Our channel was supposed to be our ministry. It was an answered prayer about my feelings of being a useless member of God's kingdom.

Since the beginning of our channel, the song *Steal My Show* by TobyMac had been my anthem and cry to God. The lines in the song that I claimed to live by were: "If You want to steal my show, I'll sit back and watch You go. If You got something to say, go on and take it away," but, sadly, I shrank back when the moment for God to take center stage finally arrived.

It wasn't without its consequences.

While I was finally living in truth in my marriage and Nia and I were thriving financially through our YouTube videos, in the background of my soul was the lingering shame of having misled our viewers in the *Forgiven* video—my response to the leaked AM account.

Once again, it appeared I had been as sick as my secrets.

The huge success we experienced over the first three years after our return paled in comparison to the challenging years after that. At the pinnacle of our YouTube career in 2017, we amassed 330 million views for the year. With each passing year, our viewership plummeted. By 2022, we could only manage to bring in 10 million views for the entire year—a 97% dip.

During our successful years, my mentor, Heath, would often encourage me to think about the longevity of our channel so that I could plan accordingly. I'd naively respond, "I think it'll last as long as we want it to."

I saw us making several hundred thousand grand a year for the rest of our lives. My high hopes turned out to be just that: high hopes. Our views tanked, and the brand deals dried up.

The realization that our primary source of income was no longer enough for us came after I paid our monthly bills one night, and it left our bank account fully depleted. Having never had a structured budget, I decided to crunch the numbers.

While keeping credit card debt below 50% of monthly income is recommended, I discovered that our credit card debt had grown to several times our monthly earnings. We had failed to adapt our lifestyle to the drastic decline in our channel, seemingly living in denial of our downfall for the previous two years. If I didn't find a job soon, I thought, it would only be a matter of time before we became insolvent.

Recent negative comments flooded my thoughts: *Your channel is dead. Why are you still posting? You guys are canceled. Your channel died fast after that baby incident, lmao. What happened to this channel?*

The truth in their words, combined with the numbers glaring back at me, sent me into an anxiety attack. Alone in a dark corner of our living room, after everyone had fallen asleep, my head fell into my hands, and I sobbed like a little boy. Worry and sadness raced through my mind.

What did I do wrong? Why wasn't I a better steward? Why us?

Then I begged God; *please don't send me back to a 9-to-5.*

It would seem I had given up on our channel, and that was why it stopped providing for us, but the truth was I had worked hard to keep it afloat, making several more large-scale project videos in an attempt to keep it alive—but it seemed I had lost my touch. They kept failing. The string of failed videos left me with creative whiplash and crippling discouragement, and I stopped giving our videos my all. The decline intensified.

I mourned that night not only for the financial uncertainty of my family's future but also for the loss of a YouTube channel that was a transformational gift from God. It restored the freedom of my creativity, rescued me from an unsatisfying career, enabled me to spend more time with my family, and gave us a platform to proclaim His name to the world. Above all, though, it acted as the catalyst that freed me from the prison of my secrets.

Our YouTube channel served our family enormously. It hurt to see it go. But what went wrong?

Could the downfall of our channel have been an indirect consequence of lying to our viewers, similar to how secrets once hindered the growth of my marriage? Could the realization that my faith wasn't as nonnegotiable as I had always believed it was cause something to break in me? Given the regret I experienced in the years that followed telling the public lies, I couldn't help but think it played a role.

I refer to the evening I filmed and uploaded *Forgiven* as *The Day I Stole from God.*

It seemed the entire world's attention was upon me for that brief moment. Yet, instead of displaying my brokenness and humbling myself before God, I let fear of man prevail. In so doing, I robbed God of the opportunity to perfect His power through my weaknesses and shine through my vulnerability.

I'm drawn to the story of Peter, who, in a moment of fear, denied knowing Jesus, and I find an unsettling resemblance in his story to mine. Although Nia's and my luxurious life had met its end, and I had seemingly blown our chance to turn *Sam and Nia* into what I always believed God intended it to be, Jesus did for me what he did for Peter; He gave me another chance.

38

The Diagnosis

I will make a pathway through the wilderness.
I will create rivers in the dry wasteland.
Isaiah 43:19

(Nia)

"ARE YOU SAYING it's my fault that my husband cheated on me?!" I asked, my voice filled with passion.

I had always been confident in my skills as a wife and was constantly reflecting on how I could improve. Although difficult to believe, Sam even reassured me over and over that I had done nothing to make him want to cheat. "If anything," he'd tell me, "I wanted more of what you were already giving me."

"Of course not, Nia," my therapist gently responded. "But you do play a part in why your marriage isn't where you want it to be."

I was beginning to get angry inside, "So what do *you* think I did wrong?"

"I'm not saying you did anything wrong," she explained. I'm saying you need to recognize that something within yourself needs to be changed."

"What needs to change in me is the constant fear that Sam is still cheating on me," I said. "Every little thing he does out of the ordinary

The Diagnosis

makes me panic inside, and I end up blowing up."

"I'm so sorry to hear that," she said. "But from that statement, it sounds like you *are* aware of how you contribute to your current situation."

"I guess so," I said.

"And the good news is," she continued, "it's within *your* power to do something about it. So let's start there: your fears. What can we do about them?"

I began telling her about my long history of fearing rejection and how Sam's betrayals had turned those fears into a reality.

"It seems like my whole life has been warning me of this nightmare I'm living in," I said.

I explained how my fears had been intensifying lately, leading me to believe they were preparing me for even more rejection ahead. My heart would pound, my hands would tremble, and my airways would tighten up at something as simple as knowing Sam was alone in a room in our house.

"Nia," she said, "I believe you have PTSD."

Her words surprised me. I hadn't been through war. How could being cheated on put me in the same category as a soldier who watched a friend die? As I learned more about the diagnosis, however, I began to embrace it.

Naming my inner turmoil gave me a way to start managing it. As my treatment began focusing on PTSD, teaching me to proactively handle it like anyone else with the diagnosis, I began to see significant improvements. The first noticeable change after dedicating myself to overcoming worry was that the triggers rarely took me by surprise anymore. When I sensed one approaching, I would stick to the plans I had put in place: Reaching out to someone in my support system, doing breathing exercises and praying, finding a quiet place and journaling my thoughts, etc.

What grounded me the most, though, was reading scripture, worshiping God, and praying. This helped me remain in the present moment and not in the worries of my future. I placed scripture cards around my house and kept worship music playing in the background all day.

One particular verse I memorized and often went back to for encouragement was Isaiah 43:18-19 which talks about God doing something new, making a "pathway through the wilderness" and "rivers in the dry wasteland."

Among the countless mental battles I faced, I needed to learn how to shield my heart from being completely shattered by any future confessions, should Sam ever have more—which there would be.

Sam's betrayals had destroyed me to my very foundation, which terrified me. I had to stop denying God, the only One who would never break His promises, His rightful place on the pedestal of my heart. Sam's spiritual leadership and love towards me were paramount in helping me make that possible.

Despite Sam's relentless efforts to support us financially through his new full-time role as a YouTube content creator while also managing the bulk of our household responsibilities, he made it a priority to become my fighting partner in my healing journey.

For months, most evenings, after kissing our children goodnight, he'd pour us each a glass of red wine, and we'd cozy up on the couch and have deep, heart-to-heart chats. We'd share what we learned during our private Bible time that day, our discipleship meetings, and our counseling sessions. We cried, laughed, and got to know each other again. We said goodbye to old habits and hello to new ones. These long conversations were huge in making me feel safe again.

Among the many new boundaries we set for our marriage, I established a particularly game-changing boundary for myself. Instead of random outbursts, I agreed that when I had a suspicion, was feeling triggered, or had a pressing question for Sam, I would warn him and plan a time to discuss it with him. This not only allowed me to cool down and gather my thoughts but also allowed Sam time to redirect his attention and prepare his heart and mind for high emotions.

Creating a new photo reel of memories in my head was also crucial to my recovery.

We took a family trip to New York City, soaking in the festive atmosphere during Christmas, where we ice skated at Rockefeller Center beneath the famous Christmas tree. "SNAP!" I took a mental image and used it to cover up a painful visual of one of Sam's confessions.

We took a road trip to the snowy mountains in New Mexico, stopping at the Grand Canyon on our way, where we enjoyed incredible views during a family bike ride. "SNAP!" I'd revisit those mental images anytime I was tempted to think about Sam riding alone in a car with another woman.

The biggest "SNAP" of all, which continues to give to this day, started when Sam and I took a trip to a small tourist town called Hochatown, Oklahoma, nestled in the heart of a national forest. While staying in a cabin there, we were inspired to purchase some property of our own. A month later, we owned a small, dilapidated home sitting on five acres of land and, over the next three years, transformed it into the cabin of our dreams, naming it *Wild Symphony* after our firstborn child. "SNAP! SNAP! SNAP!" The movie reel of betrayals that played in my head without notice was slowly being replaced.

We listed the *Wild Symphony* on Airbnb as a vacation rental cabin, which soon became our primary source of income, stepping in when our channel stopped providing enough for our family.

My journey took another significant turn in the weeks leading up to the birth of our third child, our rainbow baby, Juliet. Bringing new life into our restored marriage was the cherry on top. Juliet felt like God's reward to me—a gift so big that it seemed to fill all the remaining shadows in my life with pure light.

We chose her name with intention. *Juliet,* meaning *gift,* captures exactly what she is to us. *Elizabeth,* meaning *pledged to God,* symbolizes our commitment to surrendering our lives to Jesus. Her presence was, and still is, a constant reminder that God heard our prayers, answered them, and laid out a huge calling for our future together.

Inviting God to redeem my marriage one trigger at a time has led to a lifetime of seeing His goodness and faithfulness up close. I was finally able to look to Him as my adoring Father, and I felt nothing less than His cherished daughter.

Over the following year, my therapist's words proved to be true:

> *By acknowledging your brokenness and your need for a Savior to do what you cannot do alone, you open yourself to the One who specializes in healing. Through this, your marriage will do more than merely survive; it will thrive and glorify God. He's far from done giving you more shiny boxes.*

39
Joyful Heartache

"Return, faithless people," declares the Lord,
"for I am your husband."
Jeremiah 3:14

(Sam)

"DO YOU TRUST your husband?" The jeweler asked Nia as she marveled at the four diamond rings lined up before her. He was unaware of the underlying significance of his question, but Nia and I, meeting eyes, secretly understood.

Nia was hesitant.

We were at Zales, three months after my full confession, picking out a wedding ring to replace the one I had put on Nia's finger seven years and one month earlier. In just two hours, I would, in effect, propose to Nia once again, this time grounded in reality.

How will she answer, I wondered. *Have I regained her trust?*

As Nia gazed into my eyes, a moment stretching into what felt like an eternity while she contemplated her reply to the loaded question, the conflicting night when I first popped the big question flashed before my eyes. Nia and I had been dating for four years and four months when I finally got down on one knee.

Joyful Heartache

****

"Bebo," I said, slowly taking a knee in front of her recliner, "will you be my mom-in-law?" I proudly held out the vintage-style diamond wedding ring I had picked up at a pawn shop for $400 three days prior.

Barely acknowledging the sparkling diamond over her lap, Bebo responded with a forced, empathetic smile, almost as if she had already known my plans. After an uncomfortable pause, she said, "You need to talk to me about how you plan on taking care of her first."

I rose from the floor, embarrassed that my cute stunt hadn't unfolded as I imagined. She didn't leap from her chair in excitement, burst into tears, or pull me into a bear hug. I sat on the couch beside her, a mix of disappointment and curiosity swirling inside me.

Did I catch her at a bad time? I wondered.

We talked about my future plans, specifically when I envisioned the wedding, when I thought we'd purchase our first home, and when I planned on graduating from nursing school and getting a real job.

Bebo outlined a few basic expectations of me as her daughter's future husband. "If you promise to always make God number one in your marriage," Bebo sternly said as she held up her index finger at me, "then yes, I'll be your mom-in-law."

"Thank you, Bebo," I said. "I definitely always will." I hugged her.

"I love you, son," she said.

I sensed Bebo was holding something back. It wasn't like her not to at least giggle at my shenanigans. It was as if she knew something I didn't, perhaps something she didn't know how to express without bursting my bubble.

Could Bebo only envision a turbulent future for her only living daughter as I knelt on one knee, knowing full well that the shine of the diamond was a lie? Did she feel defeated as she realized the wisdom she wanted to give me was beyond my maturity to grasp? Maybe what she really wanted to say was, "She's just too young, and I don't trust you." Whatever it was, there was a sadness in her eyes that never left me.

When Nia arrived home from her shift at Sonic Drive-In, fifteen minutes after my conversation with Bebo, I was lying on her bed, trying to recalibrate my emotions and rehearse my proposal. In just a few minutes, I planned to ask her the most significant question of our lives.

"Hey!" Nia said excitedly as she jumped into the bed beside me.

After agreeing to go on a stroll with me, I led Nia past Bebo and out her front door into the mysterious night.

When Nia and I arrived at my pre-planned destination, an outdoor hallway at our local Baptist church where, early on in our relationship, I had promised to always be faithful to her, I found that I was much more nervous than I expected.

She turned to face me, telling me with her eyes that she'd rather be nowhere else on earth. I took a deep breath as she put her chest against mine. Staring up at me, she reached for my front jacket pocket—the same pocket where the wedding ring lay hidden.

I playfully blocked her hands from entering. "Stop!" I laughed.

Is she onto me? I wondered.

"My hands are cold!" she said.

I nervously laughed, then drew her into a hug to give her hands somewhere else to go.

"Awww, this is such a sweet hug," Nia said. "Please don't ever let go."

Phew. She doesn't hear my heart pounding, I thought. "Never," I said.

After releasing her, I looked into her eyes and maintained a nervous smile. After 30 seconds of the staring game, she giggled and asked, "What, cutie?" She absentmindedly reached for the forbidden pocket again. I clasped her hands in mine before they could enter.

"Wait!" she exclaimed. "Do you have something!?" Her words echoed through the cold, dimming-lit hallway.

I took a deep breath, blowing it out hard and fast.

"What is it!?" she demanded.

I slowly began lowering myself onto one knee in front of her, keeping my gaze locked on her face.

"Oh my gosh!" she squealed, her voice in disbelief. "What are you doing!?" She took a step back, and tears welled up in her eyes.

My hands shaking in fear, I pulled the box from my pocket and held it up to her. I snapped it open. Inside, a single LED light attached to the upper half shone a bright white glow onto the diamond ring nestled below.

"Oh my gosh! Cutie!?" she exclaimed.

I began, "God brought you and me together to create the most powerful love that this world has ever seen, and I want to spend the rest of my life working on making that love even bigger with you."

Nia started sniffling.

"I can't wait to start the next chapter of our lives together and see what God has in store for us," I continued. "There's absolutely no one else I'd rather spend the rest of my life with, and..." I stuttered, moistening my dry lips. Forgetting the rest of my rehearsed speech, I went straight to the heart of the matter.

"Will you marry me?" I asked.

"Yes!" Nia yelled, throwing her arms around my neck, nearly knocking me to the ground.

After admiring the ring together and repeating my proposal speech at Nia's request, we returned to Bebo's house, finding she had gone to bed. Nia, nervous but wanting to include Bebo in her big moment, entered her bedroom and, from her bedside, told her the news.

"I'm so happy for you, Sug!" I overheard Bebo say as I sat alone on Nia's bed.

I couldn't help but think Bebo had gone to bed early with a broken heart, hoping to avoid the reality that her baby had grown up and would soon be moving out, leaving her to live alone.

It was a bittersweet evening for all of us, seemingly more bitter than sweet for Bebo. Nia and I were eager to start sharing a pillow and live under the same roof, yet we couldn't help but feel sad for Bebo. In a mix of emotions, Nia laid her head on my chest and got teary-eyed. The moment felt distinctly unnatural. All I could imagine was Bebo crying into her pillow alone.

I silently prayed that Nia would never end up in the lonely position that Bebo found herself in. *Please go ahead of us, Lord, and protect our marriage from divorce,* I begged. *This isn't how You intended this moment to be.* Bebo should have had a husband to share the moment with and comfort her. *God, please be that husband for Bebo.*

Nine months later, Nia and I tied the knot, moved into our newly purchased home, and conceived our first child. Bebo all the while being the sweetest mom-in-law a man could ever ask for.

****

Looking into my eyes, Nia finally replied to the jeweler, "Yeah."

My heart leaped for joy.

Four months had passed since I first turned Nia's world upside down. Although it would be years before I completely regained her trust, hearing that she even trusted my opinion on which diamond ring suited her best—whether she said it just to appease the jeweler or not—felt like a significant accomplishment, one I could only credit to God.

Nia left Zales sparkling; I left encouraged.

An hour later, at a large display fountain in the center of an outdoor mall, I slipped the new ring onto Nia's finger and then, from my phone, read to her:

God has given us a second chance... I come today to give you my love, to give you my heart and my hope for our future together... I promise there will never be a single person on this earth that I will choose over you, including myself, ever again. I promise I will live first for God rather than myself or even you. I promise that I will lead our family into a life of faith in Jesus. And No matter what may lie ahead of us, I pledge to you my life as a loving and faithful husband.

As we stood at this turning point, wanting so badly to take a peaceful stroll into the sunset, I knew that the path God was charting for us behind the scenes would continue to require us to venture into the uncomfortable unknown.

"I know we still have a lot of work ahead of us," I added, "The good work He's begun in us is far from complete."

40

We Can't Rewind

And though a man might prevail against one who is alone, two will withstand him—a threefold cord is not quickly broken.
Ecclesiastes 4:12

(Nia)

"SAM AND NIA," Pastor Bo began, "ten years ago, when you first joined hands, hearts, and souls, you didn't know where the path would take you. And it's been quite a ride. Ups that were extremely high, and are still high, and downs that were very low."

"I mean, who knew," Pastor Bo continued with a smile, "that so much would come out of *Love is an Open Door,* right?" Everyone laughed.

It was September 21st, 2019, a gorgeous fall evening with no rain clouds in sight. I can still smell the freshly cut flowers mixed with the catered Greek cuisine and feel the gentle breeze caressing my face.

While Andrea, my sister-in-law, styled my hair, I watched my friend Lauren, the mastermind behind our wedding vow renewal, set up the centerpieces on each of the ten round tables arranged on the bright green lawn that would soon be filled by the people we love most.

My heart was full.

Among our guests were Heath and Chantel, two pillars in our lives who had, without realizing it, prepared us for the most important fight of our lives. They shared heartfelt toasts during the reception, touching everyone's hearts.

Sam's brother Matthew walked around with his camera, just like he had on our wedding day, capturing stunning photos, one of which would become the cover of this book. He also gave an emotional toast to Sam and me, cleverly starting it with a line from Disney's Frozen: "Can I say something crazy?"

The ceremony began with Sam walking our two girls, Symphony and Juliet, dressed in lacy white dresses, down to the altar. There, they would wait for me to walk down the aisle for the second time, escorted by Abram, our six-year-old son.

As Sam came into view, my heart began to race. This processional, in contrast to my first, felt richer. We didn't know what we didn't know a decade ago, but there had been so much spiritual growth and wisdom gained since then that it was almost palpable.

This time, we knew who each other was, as well as ourselves, on a much deeper and spiritual level, knowing more precisely what we were getting into. Jesus had become each of our *only* foundations. No longer did we share each other with His place in our lives. We had always belonged to each other, but it wasn't until the past several years that we really got to know our *oneness*, God being the glue that held us together. We learned that maintaining our covenant meant maintaining good communication and living in close community with other believers.

As I closed the distance between us, walking towards Sam through all the people who we couldn't have done it without, keeping our eyes locked on each other, we both agreed without saying a word; w*e're still a team hard to beat.*

Abram handed me off to his dad, who wasn't as much a ball of emotions as he was on our first wedding day but instead looked like a stronger and wiser version of him. Abram stood beside us with Juliet and Symphony, enjoying our public recommitment to each other as a family. Renewing our vows was also for them.

"Both of you look at me for just one second," Bo said to Sam and me midway through his heartfelt message. "I *know* that God is pleased with you. I *know* that He is proud of you." His words had us both reaching for tissue.

Sam began his new vows to me by acknowledging the old ones. While all his words to me were incredibly meaningful, the fact that he started there meant the most to me. After so many years, God was, once again, unexpectedly redeeming another trigger for me.

"On our wedding day, I pledged many things to you, including my fidelity," Sam said. "With sorrow and remorse, and sometimes feeling like a total idiot, I acknowledge that I broke that vow."

As Sam continued to read, his eyes filled with tears, God gave me a vivid mental image of his old vows at the altar of our first wedding, slowly transitioning into the present moment.

"I pledge myself and my faith to you until death do us part," Sam continued. "I promise to keep myself open to you, to let you see into my soul. From this day forward, I will guard my transformed heart for you and foremost for the God we both fear."

Had I never given God the chance to do his healing work in our marriage, someone else might have been enjoying the benefits of the changed man standing before me. I was overcome with thankfulness to have stuck it out with him. What a reward!

I unfolded my vows, handed to me by Abram, and began reading, "I give all glory to God for holding our hands these past few years and showing me how to keep my vows when things have been really, really hard."

Throughout the previous ten years, we had, individually and as a couple, surrendered complete control of our lives to God; I would no longer be responsible for preventing Sam from straying; I would leave that in God's hands. Similarly, it wouldn't be Sam's responsibility to remove himself from the pedestal I had placed him on; that would be between me and God. Just the same, it would be God who would sustain Sam as he walked in his new life of freedom from his secrets and struggles.

As the wedding reception began, Sam and I took center stage for our second *first* dance, this time to the song, *Do You Remember* by Jack Johnson. The song's first lines filled the air, "Do you remember when we first met? I sure do; it was sometime in early September..."

Sam's hand gripped my waist, the other holding my hand outstretched, as we moved at a pace double that of our original first dance. This was the beginning of a journey we were excited to continue with joy and resilience.

Inches from each other's faces, we sang along with the song's final stanza: "Over ten years have gone by. We can't rewind. We're locked in time. But you're still mine. Do you remember?"

We were committed to being fully open and honest with each other even when the truth was ugly. This time, however, the burden of our battles did not rest solely on our shoulders. As "a cord of three strands is not easily broken," God had officially and permanently become our marriage's most important and strongest member.

With God on our side, we felt equipped to face any trial. But as we looked ahead, a question remained: What kind of work would this new chapter bring, and were we as ready as we felt we were? It would soon become clear that what God wanted from us next was beyond our courage to do alone.

41

Fully Exposed

Blows that wound cleanse away evil;
Strokes make clean the innermost parts.
Proverbs 20:30

(Sam)

SIX AND A half years after baring my flesh and soul to Nia, I found myself seated at a round table with four other men wrestling with sexual brokenness. A meeting of *BOLD* (Brothers Overcoming Lustful Desires) Ministry was in session.

"God will turn what once held you captive into a tool to defeat the enemy," Bryan Stewart, the ministry's founder, said. "We are *more* than conquerors, men!"

After Bryan finished his message, a group member raised his hand. He took the mic and said, "Guys, there's power in transparency. Jesus hung on the cross completely naked, vulnerable, and exposed for the sake of His church. He made the ultimate sacrifice for His bride. We've got to be willing to do the same for our wives."

His statement struck me as one of the most beautiful things I ever heard. I wanted to jump onto the table and scream, "Amen!" I was right where I belonged, among other men unafraid to confront the truth, regardless of difficulty, all in pursuit of becoming better husbands and stronger men of God.

Echoing Pontius Pilate's timeless question to Jesus, "What is truth?" Since that fateful drive in Seattle, my ears have been open to understanding more of that elusive answer every day. Seeking truth became the risky adventure I always craved.

I'm no philosopher, but who was I to think I could change reality? How could I begin to solve my problem of discontentment if I was afraid to look at myself honestly? If I was maintaining lies, thinking it was protecting myself or others, what other lies might I be unintentionally believing, and could those lies be destroying me? I had once lived a lie; now, I'd strive to do the exact opposite for the rest of my life.

Shortly after joining *BOLD*, Bryan mentioned I was an ideal fit for leadership. "We're most qualified to help the people we used to be," he said, trying to convince me when he saw the hesitation in my face.

The old me would have fled at the word "leadership," probably mostly because of the shame I had been carrying around with me. But having been set free from my snare and tasting the sweetness of God's goodness, I was compelled to take Bryan up on his offer to help other men.

During a Sunday evening meeting, while leading a discussion on the *FASTER scale*, a tool that helps men identify when they might be on the verge of a relapse, I saw a reflection of who I used to be in a young man sitting across from me.

He confessed to the group that his wife had recently discovered his unfaithfulness and was struggling with the realization that his identity could not be found in women, including his wife. He didn't know who he was. The affair didn't satisfy him as he thought it would, but he was enduring repercussions that seemed impossible to fix.

On my way home that night, I extended the same simple offer to him that Heath had made to me nearly ten years earlier, beginning the relationship that transformed my life.

"Hey man," I texted, "it's Sam Rader from *BOLD*. Wanna grab coffee sometime?"

A year into regular meetings with this hungry man of God, where I challenged him in his newfound identity in Jesus and supported him through the healing journey of his marriage, he shared with me that our time together had been a pivotal reason he managed to keep his family afloat. He and his wife now share a marriage that once seemed beyond the realm of possibility for them.

I excitedly and with the utmost honor accepted that God's plan for the rest of my life was to disciple one sexually broken man at a time, supporting them in courageously living in truth.

It felt incredibly rewarding to finally be part of the solution to adultery rather than part of the problem. Mere months later, we received a life-changing email that took Nia's and my passion for bringing hope to other struggling marriages to a level that was unimaginable for us.

42

Leaving Home

And I am sure of this, that he who began a good work in you will bring it to completion at the day of Jesus Christ.
Philippians 1:6

(Nia)

"I THINK IT'S time we start looking for a new church," Sam said.

For over seven years, I waited to understand what the Lord meant when He told me at the baby shower that Sam and I would be in marriage ministry together. Year after year passed, and no opportunities presented themselves.

Just as I began to second-guess what I heard from the Lord in 2021, six years after the baby shower moment, something unexpected started to stir in our hearts.

"I feel like we need to get out of our comfort zone," Sam continued. "And I really want *more* church."

I *liked* that my church home was comfortable and risk-free, so when Sam first brought this same idea to me several months earlier, my response was stern: "No way. I'll never leave this Church." I appreciated Sam's adventurous personality, but I wasn't going to let it come between me and the people who locked arms with us during the most difficult time of our lives.

"We've served this church faithfully for a decade now, cutie," Sam said. "I think it's time."

I wanted to argue that we shouldn't give up when the going gets tough, but it wasn't something I could claim this time. Our mentors, Bo, Chantel, and Heath, had all moved away to distant cities over a year earlier. That was when things got the most difficult for us, and we didn't quit then.

"The last thing I want for us is to settle in our walk," he added. Among the concerns Sam raised, one of the most significant to me was that Symphony wouldn't have a youth group to join once she was old enough.

Despite my fear of potentially leaving behind the people who were instrumental in our transformation, I trusted Sam as the spiritual leader of our home. So, I finally told him, "I'm open to praying about it with you."

After extensive prayer and multiple discussions with mentors, family, and our church leaders, Sam and I decided to move on from the comfort of our "mother" church and step out in faith toward the "more church" that Sam believed God was calling us to.

Our search soon led us to Lakeshore, a church just a few miles from where we lived. On our first visit, it happened to be Lakeshore's bi-annual *Small Group Sunday*.

As Sam and I walked around the foyer after dropping our children off at the kid's church, I was drawn to a table marked *Women*. This was where I learned about *BOLD for Women*. The group's description read, "Designed to help women dealing with the fallout of broken vows or trust."

"So what did you think?" Sam asked as we exited Lakeshore's parking lot after the service.

"I don't want to be dramatic, but I think I could cry," I said.

Sam laughed.

"I really feel like this is our new church home," I added.

Within a month, we were active members of Lakeshore.

I immediately got plugged into *BOLD for Weomen,* comforting as many women as possible by showing them they weren't alone in their healing journey. It soon became clear that when God whispered "marriage ministry" to me, He meant exactly what He said. Also, the "more church" that Sam felt God was pushing him toward began to make perfect sense to us.

Our previous church had raised us well, thoroughly preparing us for this integral and complex chapter of our lives that came next. We wouldn't have been able to say "yes" to half the things that came our way hadn't it been for the people at Reach.

Amber Stewart—the leader of *BOLD Women*—and I shared an equal passion for using what God had done in our marriages to fight alongside other women. She and I would go on to create our own recovery curriculum together, which we'd use to facilitate the *BOLD Women* meetings.

In my difficult journey to marriage ministry, I learned a lesson about trust and God's timing. God desired for me to prove my trust in Him across all aspects of my life before He'd unveil the big blessings He had for me. James speaks to this in chapter one: "Consider it pure joy, my brothers and sisters, whenever you face trials of many kinds, because you know that the testing of your faith produces perseverance."

Perseverance, among the many other Christian virtues I grew in along the way, was more than necessary for me to do my job well in marriage ministry.

Watching how powerfully God continues to use my sufferings to help other women, allowing them to use my victories as their very own weapons against the enemy, I can now confidently say—however crazy it sounds—that if given the chance, I wouldn't change a single part of my past.

43
Final Confession

My grace is sufficient for you, for my power is made perfect in weakness."
Therefore I will boast all the more gladly of my weaknesses, so that the power of Christ may rest upon me.
2 Corinthians 12:9

(Sam)

"HERE, SAM, TAKE this," Zoe, the producer, said, handing me an iPad.

"Oh no," I responded as I caught a glimpse of my face on the screen. "How did you even get this?"

"The internet never forgets," she replied.

It was my *Forgiven* video, in which I told our YouTube audience I would never mention my Ashley Madison account again.

In February 2023, Minnow Films, Netflix, and ourselves entered into a contract. This agreement was not only an opportunity for me to finally confess the lies I told and clear my conscience once and for all but also for Nia and me to share with the world how God rescued our marriage.

As I watched the *Forgiven* video for the first time since uploading it eight years prior, I quickly realized my deceptions had been far worse than I remembered. I watched in disbelief as I told lie after lie, even resorting to God to make my lies more believable. The fear in the eyes of the man looking back at me was unsettling. I wanted to grab him by the shoulders and say, "Dude! Shut up already!"

I watched on as a man who looked exactly like me hollowed himself out, throwing out substance with each lie. It was gut-wrenching, an indescribable experience, watching myself fabricate lies just to protect my brief reputation on earth. At the same time, however, it was a beautiful reminder.

It would have been easy to give into my initial desires to throw the iPad at my garage door, storm out, and wallow in regret, but the contrast between who I saw in the video and the person I was while watching it was worth celebrating. I had been set free from that prison! Exonerated! Redeemed! And there I sat in the huge opportunity of stepping out of the darkness once again.

"If you were so afraid to tell the truth when the hack took place," Toby began, "why are you willing to be so truthful now?"

"Because His grace is finally enough for me," I said.

Toby nodded his head hurriedly. It clearly wasn't the response he wanted, but I continued.

"His power is made perfect in my weakness," I added.

"Thank you, Sam," Toby replied, giving a thumbs up.

"Therefore, I will boast all the more gladly of my weaknesses so the power of Christ may rest upon me."

Toby later told me my quoted scripture didn't make the final cut. While I had hoped this personal favorite would be included, and despite earlier concerns that Netflix might omit Jesus from our story altogether, I was no longer worried.

"There's just no way Netflix is going to share the redemptive part of your story," a friend would try to warn me. "Based on their track record of trying to make Christians look like idiots, it makes no sense."

"All the more reason to just trust God," I replied. "Either way, He's going to use it."

No matter how Nia and I are portrayed in the AM docuseries, we knew that sitting in front of their cameras was God's will for us.

The Bible says, "Has the LORD redeemed you? Then speak out!" and that is what we did. Besides, Nia and I had grown to care deeply about Toby and Zoe; we were grateful that they, along with everyone else on the Minnow Films team, heard our redemptive story in its entirety.

That night, Nia and I prayed together, asking God that if nothing else came from all our interviews, the transformative work He had done in our lives would touch at least one receptive heart among those who heard about it during the production process.

44
Once a Cheater

*He is like a tree planted by streams of water that
yields its fruit in its season, and its leaf does not wither.
In all that he does, he prospers.*
Psalm 1:3

(Nia)

ON A SUNNY September afternoon in 2022, I put my hair up in my fancy date-night bun and did my favorite makeup routine, then joined Sam on the bed, where he sat in front of his open laptop.

"Wow, look at you," Sam said flirtatiously.

"Two random women are about to learn that you cheated on me," I said, partially kidding. "I want to look my best."

"Can I at least take you on a date after this?" he asked.

"You better," I said, giving him a peck on the lips before snuggling in at his side.

We had a video call scheduled with the casting directors, Claire and Amanda from Minnow Films. The topic was Sam's involvement in the 2015 Ashley Madison breach and our interest in participating in the docuseries they were creating for Netflix. I thought I had mentally prepared for everything they would ask until, midway through, Claire threw us a curveball. "Has there been unfaithfulness in your marriage since the confessions in Seattle?" she asked.

Sam and I froze. The moment triggered the panicky emotions I'd get before one of Sam's confessions. As Sam and I looked into each other's wide eyes with uncomfortable grins, unsure of how much the other was willing to share, my mind drifted to calculating how long it had been since his last confession. It had been about a year.

"Yes," Sam admitted, "I have had to confess other slip-ups with her."

"Would you mind sharing a bit more about that?" Claire asked. I braced myself for the unexpected. I'd grown to learn that Sam wouldn't allow fear to come between him and the truth again. Still, I wasn't immune to it.

"It's only been a handful of times," Sam began. "mostly involving pornography or other women getting in my head. Things like that."

Sam had remained open and vulnerable with me as he promised he would. For example, several months later, he would tell me he stopped visiting a coffee shop because he felt attracted to a barista there. Over the years, the time between confessions grew progressively wider and the slip-ups less severe, but my immediate reaction to them seemed to remain the same. Taking a deep breath before speaking was usually enough to re-ground me.

After our video call ended, Sam and I stayed on the bed while processing the emotional two-hour interview.

"Was it just me, or did Amanda seem really moved when you talked about forgiveness?" Sam asked.

"Yeah, she really did," I replied, trying to find the right moment to ask what was really on my mind.

"I feel like that went pretty good," he said.

"Is this a good time to ask you a question?" I suddenly asked.

Sam chuckled. "I suppose," he said, knowing from experience what was coming.

I repositioned myself on the bed in front of him. "So?" I asked.

"What?" he asked with more nervous laughter.

"If there's anything you need to get off your chest before we continue with this whole documentary thing," I said, "now is the time to do it." Sam stretched his arms above his head and took a deep breath, tell-tale signs he had something uncomfortable to say. "Just tell me," I said.

"A couple weeks ago I sat near a girl at Starbucks and made friendly small talk with her." He said. "It was nothing."

"Okay?" I said, my heart rate increasing.

"She was reading a finance book that I've read before, and I just gave her some random investment advice," he added.

"How long did you talk to her?" I asked.

"Maybe ten minutes off and on," he said.

"Did you get her number?" I asked, half joking.

"No," he said. "I didn't get her number, but…" He paused, shaking his head. *Oh great,* I thought, *here we go.* He continued, "When she walked out, I waved goodbye to her kind of flirtatiously, and she smiled back at me."Disappointment struck me. He continued to confess that he had allowed his mind to fantasize about her but told me he had quickly taken the thoughts to the Lord, after which he said they went away. He told me he never saw her again. "It's so dumb," he added. "I'm so sorry."

"I need a minute," I told him as I got up and left the room. "Don't come after me." I went straight to my Bible and sat in our backyard. After a minute of praying and controlled breathing, I noticed something distinctly different going on inside me. Although I was upset and felt I could boil over if I wanted to, Sam's confession didn't make it to my core and wreck me as they usually did. My peace was still within reach.

I opened up my Bible to the first chapter of Psalms and began reading:

> *Oh, the joys of those who do not follow the advice of the wicked… But they delight in the law of the Lord, meditating on it day and night. They are like trees planted along the riverbank, bearing fruit each season. Their leaves never wither, and they prosper in all they do.*

The words were a breath of fresh air. I realized that was exactly what I had become in making God number one in my life: a tree on the riverbank. My roots ran too deep for another person's decision to uproot me. It then occurred to me that two years earlier, unrelated to Sam's struggles, my faith had come to my rescue in a similar way. I often revisited that day, believing it reflected what God had accomplished in my marriage.

****

March 9th, 2021, was a date I had carefully planned and prepared for. I was scheduled to give birth to our fourth child. I did everything possible to organize our home and complete the to-do lists in hopes of improving my chances of warding off postpartum depression if it decided it wanted to make another appearance in my life. However, I may have never bothered trying if I knew the number of things that would soon go wrong.

For starters, COVID safety measures were in effect. No one besides Sam was allowed to visit at any point during my hospital stay. On top of the isolation, I was more nervous and emotional about the procedures that awaited me than I had been with any of my other pregnancies. I needed my girlfriends by my side more than ever, but I couldn't have them.

My state of mind alone had me worried I was bound for postpartum depression again. I was stuck in a cycle of fear. I remembered the prayer that was said over me the previous Sunday; "W*e declare that no weapon formed against Nia, including depression, shall prosper."* I prayed it again.

I sat on the edge of a bed, my back arched in a freezing hospital room, my doctor holding my legs down as I grasped her forearms in a death grip. *God, help me,* I prayed. *Help me through this last time that a needle will be shoved into my spine.*

As the anesthetic kicked in, numbing everything below my chest, the nurses rolled me into the operating room, where I was met with a surprise. It was Sam making a surgical gown look good and holding a camera as usual.

"Hey, cutie," he said.

"Oh my gosh, hey!" I said as tears jumped out of my eyes. He covered my forehead with his hand and looked down at me. "Do you still think it's a boy?" I asked.

"Whatever it is," he said, "I can't wait to meet him." He made me laugh, easing my nerves.

Before I knew it, after hearing my doctor say, "Well, hello, darling," our baby was born.

"It's a girl!" a nurse announced.

"No way!" I exclaimed. "It's a girl?" Tears filled my eyes as my baby girl's first cries went into my ears and straight to my heart. After Sam snipped off her umbilical cord, Josie Grace Rader was placed on my chest. Her scent was sweeter than any flower I had ever smelled, instantly filling me with peace.

How could I be so blessed, I thought. *Thank you, Lord.*

The new life in my arms brought me back to reality and far away from my anxieties. Ten minutes later, however, I began to feel sharp abdominal pains, and the atmosphere in the operating room shifted to one of urgency. Josie was taken off my chest and handed to Sam.

"Cancel my next appointment," I overheard my doctor tell her assistant.

"Is everything okay, doctor?" I mumbled as a wave of nausea came over me.

"Honey, your bladder was really stuck, and there's a tiny hole in it, and I can't find it," my doctor casually replied. My heart started beating so fast that I thought I might vomit it out of my body. As an oxygen mask was placed over my face, a nurse instructed Sam to leave the room with Josie. I was alone and anxious all over again. Then suddenly, everything went black.

An hour later, after another doctor entered the scene and the nick in my bladder was located and repaired, I began to wake up. I was wheeled back to my room and greeted by Sam and my new baby girl. I could finally start breastfeeding her.

As I nourished her, I felt a deep, almost spiritual bond form between us. It not only calmed her but also soothed my own soul. The skin-to-skin touch, our eye contact, and her fresh scent made the world around me disappear. The worst of the delivery was behind me.

The following day, my nurse came into my room with more bad news: "Josie is losing too much weight." I was immediately concerned for Josie and frustrated that I wasn't producing enough milk for her. My lactation consultant had me begin supplementing her feedings with formula, something I wanted to avoid. My dream of breastfeeding my last baby was at risk of being crushed. I was really bracing for postpartum depression now.

After a five-day extended hospital stay, after talks of Josie having to possibly stay behind in the NICU for her lack of weight gain, we were finally discharged. Along with the three of us, however, I arrived home with a Foley catheter still in place and several scheduled appointments to monitor Josie's weight and my bladder repair.

Nestled in our king-sized bed a week later as a family of six for the first time, we took turns cradling our tiny Josie, dressed in thin pajamas and wrapped in a fluffy blanket. Gazing down at her, staring into her tired, brown eyes, my mind wandered back to all the complications we had endured together.

The challenges of my delivery felt like a perfect storm, sure to lead to postpartum depression. Yet, as I looked at the new life in my arms, I was only hopeful. There were no dark thoughts in sight. I glanced at a pile of laundry overflowing in our hamper to be sure... only a smile came to my face. *Thank you for your protection,* I prayed. *And thank you for new life.*

****

Even when Sam's Starbucks confession suddenly dropped me into a windstorm, I remained firmly rooted. I was an evergreen planted by a flowing river that contained all the nutrients a tree could ever need and more, strengthening me for moments like these and the other storms that would surely come my way.

I went back into our bedroom and told Sam I forgave him. I wouldn't always be so gracious, but thankfully, I was in fruit-bearing season, and this storm hadn't been strong enough to blow *all* my fruit off the tree. The fruits that remained were self-control, quick forgiveness, thankfulness for Sam's honesty, and love for the amazing reminder that my joy was deeply rooted and never without supply.

"Now," I said playfully, "if you ever want to sit next to me again, you better be careful where you sit in public."

Ten months later, I sat before Netflix cameras and completed my final interview for their Ashley Madison docuseries. It was a relief to have it behind me, but not for reasons I would have expected. Revisiting the most challenging period of my life in such detail was surprisingly cathartic. As I had told my best friends the day after, "I didn't know there was any more redemption in this story to be had."

The in-depth conversations with Zoe, the producer who interviewed me, helped me see all the areas where God had brought complete restoration to my life. Instead of feeling triggered after the interview, I found myself full of thankfulness and praising God.

Surprised and a little worried about how it would come across that I got through most of the interview without shedding a tear, I asked Zoe, "Did I look disconnected?"

"Oh no," she said. "The camera guy even remarked how great your interview went. He hasn't said that about anyone."

"Aww, thank you, Zoe," I said.

"Your strength is what shone through, not a lack of emotion or warmth," she added.

Over the following weeks, giving God the glory for how well my interview went, I couldn't help but wonder what it was that the Minnow Films crew, seemingly all non-Christians, saw in me. Even the executive producer, Fiona, would reach out months after my interview to tell me with genuine emotion in her eyes, "You come across as a really strong, grounded person." The whole crew seemed genuinely thankful to have been a part of my testimony, and I wasn't going to write it off as mere professionalism.

"You were brilliant, Nia," the director Toby told me on multiple occasions.

I wanted to put a finger on it. *What did they see?* I wondered. Then, I remembered.

The production team saw a tree being fed by the richest water, the storms of her past having only made her roots grow deeper and stronger. This tree had a source that they were unfamiliar with but was undeniably powerful. They saw a tree whose leaves surprisingly would never wither, yielding the purest kind of fruit, which they probably couldn't help but want for themselves. They saw a woman rooted in the Savior of the world, a tree on the riverbank, with no end to its prosperity in sight.

45

Ultimate Romance

*For as a young man marries a young woman,
so shall your sons marry you, and as the bridegroom
rejoices over the bride, so shall your God rejoice over you.
Isaiah 62:5*

(Sam)

"NOW THAT WE'RE nearing the end of our interview," said Toby, the director, perched on a stool in my garage, two bulky Netflix cameras capturing every detail of my expressions, "how would you say your perception of reality versus fantasy has changed since your confessions to Nia?"

I paused to consider his question.

"There's a line in the movie *Big Fish,*" I began, "that only recently stood out to me after seeing it at least 20 times. A woman asks Edward Bloom, who is now on his deathbed, if it's his medication that's been making him so thirsty lately. Edward Bloom responds by saying, 'The truth is I've been thirsty my whole life, and I've never really known why.' I had always related to Edward Bloom, but when I finally caught this, I felt sorry for him."

"Like me," I continued, "he had been trying to satisfy himself with women and other ventures his whole life, but unlike me, he was going to die before drinking the water that would allow him to never thirst again."

Toby gave a thumbs up. He knew where I was headed.

"All that's to say," I added, "I feel bad for the old me who believed in fantasies, and I regret all the damage that was caused because of it, but I'm thankful that I'm now living in truth and no longer have that unquenchable thirst."

After the seven-hour, emotionally exhausting Netflix interview in my hot garage, which felt more like a never-ending counseling session, I fell onto our bed beside Nia. "I can't believe five strangers now know every sleazy detail of my past," I said, "let alone the whole world soon knowing." Nia and I shared a boisterous laugh, trying to shake off our nervous tension.

I turned to her and met her eyes. "I really am so sorry for everything I put you through," I said.

"Aww, thank you, Sammy," she replied. "I *guess* I forgive you," she added with a cheeky smile.

As we silently looked into each other's eyes, I was reminded of the terrifying yet life-changing day when God first asked me to share my testimony publicly. *Was this Netflix interview the moment He had been preparing me for?* I wondered.

"What are you thinking about?" Nia asked, as she always did when she caught me drifting into one of my notorious trances.

****

For the first time in ages, I skipped breakfast and my morning cup of coffee—not because I wasn't hungry, but because my stomach felt twisted and off-limits with adrenaline levels already too high.

"Listen up, gentlemen," the host of our church-wide men's retreat announced. "Sam Rader is coming up to share his testimony with us."

To this day, my best friend Erick teases me about the nervous cough I developed during our high school speech class. He'd never seen anyone with worse stage fright than me, nor had I. Yet there I was, a grown version of the boy who was never even able to converse with his father without fearing he'd be ridiculed, about to share my deepest thoughts with a room full of grown men.

To the applause of my formidable audience, I stepped in front of the mic, my hands and legs trembling. *Tell them you can't do it,* I thought. *Tell them you're sick, anything, just save yourself.*

I cleared my throat. "As you'll see..." my voice cracked, "I'm a YouTuber, *not* a public speaker." The room broke out in laughter as I took in a deep breath. *Don't you dare cough again,* I told myself before saying, "And unfortunately, I won't be able to edit out the cringey moments for you like I do for our viewers."

Over the next 40 minutes, I fumbled through my testimony of how God delivered me from a life shrouded in secrets to one rooted in truth. I concluded it by confessing that, despite this transformation, I currently felt depressed and distanced from God once again. "But this time," I added, "there are no secrets. I'm an open book with my wife and anyone else who cares to listen." After the group said a prayer over me, I returned to my comfortable seat in the back and felt God's loving pat on my back.

I survived. Thank you, Lord.

As the men's retreat drew to a close, each man was handed a manila envelope containing letters of encouragement from loved ones. I found a secluded spot outside on the grass and pulled out the first letter. It was from Pastor Bo.

"You have been through the refiner's fire," he wrote, "and come out the other side a much better man than you were ten years ago." As I read his heartfelt letter, I was flooded with thankfulness for having such a steadfast man of God in my life whom I could call a friend. He concluded the letter with a prayer: "More than any of the fun at this men's retreat, I pray that God will speak a word to your heart that will help you draw closer to Him and navigate life's rapids... I love you, brother." His prayer for me was mere minutes away from being answered.

The next letter I pulled out was from my brother Matthew. "I've been inspired by the way you have grown in the Lord," he wrote. "The way you have loved your wife and family has been a model for me to do the same in my marriage; thank you for that." I felt humbled that the redeemed life that God allowed me to live could be an encouragement to my older and wiser brother, who had consistently supported my family over the years. My heart was full.

I slid the next letter out of the envelope. It began with, "Dear Sammy." I immediately knew it was from my incredible wife. I suddenly felt giddy inside. I was on the precipice of reading the "word for my heart" that Bo had prayed I'd receive.

She wrote:

> *It feels so different to be typing you a letter like this. We haven't communicated in written form, other than texting, in years. And before that, all we had were written notes.*

Those notes were passed between immature and insecure people, and today, it's being passed between a man and a woman after God's heart. How amazing! I've been thinking a lot about your connection to movies and big love stories like in Big Fish and Moulin Rouge... Don't ever forget that the way you view those relationships is very likely the way God looks at you. He sees you with that Big Fish kind of love... I imagine you being the one inside the window, Him yelling your name instead of Sandra's .... "Samuel Rader! I love you, and I WILL marry you!"

Tears fell onto her letter like I had suddenly put it under a running faucet. I was awestruck by her wisdom. Before reading on, I sat in tears, trying to grasp the enormous significance of how she had just flipped my favorite movie line into one of the most profound sentences I've ever read.

God wants to marry ME!? I wondered.

Big Fish by Tim Burton was my all-time favorite movie. I even printed out the script when it was released in 2003 and committed to heart all the lines that spoke to me. A year after its release, just a week into our relationship, I shouted from a moving car to Nia as she practiced with her color guard team in our high school parking lot, "NiaChel Rand! I love you, and I *will* marry you!" She was my Sandra Templeton.

In a seemingly sacrificial act, putting it in writing, Nia officially demoted herself from the primary role in my life. *She's trying to protect me from falling for a fantasy again,* I concluded, a*t the cost of herself.*

Her words were a selfless effort to encourage me not to let her beauty define my worth and not to allow our romance to distract me from the ultimate romance above. She wanted me to have what she had: a profound, soul-defining relationship filled with boundless intimacy, grace and forgiveness, and perfect love with the ultimate Bridegroom. I couldn't think of a bigger gesture of love than this.

I reflected on how, over the years, Nia helped me see why Hollywood love stories usually end at the wedding: romance, in the long run, isn't glamorous when it's made to be the ultimate thing. As it turns out, marriage isn't the climax of life, and our spouses can't redeem us.

As I rubbed my eyes, I replayed Nia's words of wisdom: *Jesus is yelling your name instead of Sandra's. "Samuel Rader! I love you, and*

I WILL marry you! This time, the words felt like they were coming from God.

Marry me, Samuel. Only I can bear the weight of your brokenness and wash you white as snow. No other relationship can carry you as I can. No one else but I have paid the price to make you my perfect bride.

The words reached into my chest and massaged my heart as if I were reliving the moment Bo told me to "live in truth" all over again. My romance with Nia had always been a mere *hint* at what the God of the universe wanted with me. No woman, YouTube audience, career, or anything else under the sun could ever quench my thirst like being betrothed to the Savior of the world.

If I could grasp this at my core, all pressure to define my identity through worldly achievements would disappear. I could pursue any path without fear or complaint. I could be a husband and father without being paralyzed by my inadequacies. I could stand before an audience of men or even share the depths of my brokenness with the world on Netflix without fearing rejection. I could even return to ER nursing or, for that matter, make a living flipping burgers and still have limitless joy and thankfulness in my heart.

How do you love me so much, Lord? I asked. *How could I have ever cheated on You? Thank you for sending Jesus so I can still be Your bride even after all my unfaithfulness. Keep me far away from the adultery that nailed Him to the cross. I want no part in any of it.*

I felt my depression easing and the distance between us closing.

Another lifelong adventure began that day: walking in God's matrimonial love for me.

****

"Tell me, or else," Nia repeated, gripping my side in a threat to tickle me.

"I was just thinking about the letter you wrote me for that men's retreat," I said shyly.

"Aww, cutie!? Again?" she said. "It's so sweet how much that letter meant to you."

Tears immediately welled up in my eyes. "I'm blown away by how you not only forgave me for so much but continue to build me up," I mumbled.

"Stop that," Nia said, blushing.

As she scooted closer and wrapped her arms around me, I recalled the rest of her letter while we held each other tight.

Marriage is a word for covenant...promise. And that's the deep and unending and even euphoric love that He has to offer you.

Something else I've been so impressed by in the last six months or so is how you aren't afraid to face your sins head-on and deal with them. I think most people take their entire lives working towards that type of commitment to Jesus and sadly, I don't think many actually achieve it. You have a real relationship with God and with Jesus and it's so apparent in how you go about life. The phrase "relationship with Jesus" can seem so vague. If someone doesn't know what that means... they are left wondering "How do I get it and what would it even look like for me?" I would say that they could look at your example and get a great idea of where to start.

I love you and I really am so proud of you, Sam. As my husband, I'm proud of how you face reality with me so kindly and willingly and lead me to Jesus. Thank you for that. As hard as things can get between us sometimes, it's not lost on me that you are always there for me, loving me, and trying to keep our marriage safe and whole.

As my friend, I'm proud of the way you study and allow the wisdom of God to guide you vs. your own way... even to the point of giving up things that most others would never be willing to do. As my lover, well... you know. But really, I have seen such a shift in the way you love me intimately compared to how things were in the first half of our marriage. I feel so treasured by you in that way. Thank you. As the father of my children, I'm so proud of the way you teach them and protect them and lead them to Jesus. And as my brother in Christ, I am so proud of the life you are living, wide open, boldly pointing to Him.